Comments

This book should stimulate a powerful movement down the road to a just peace. It is a must read, especially for Americans who have no Arab ancestry. Through fascinating personal interviews with Arabs in private life in the Middle East, this book identifies a shocking made-in-America Ground Zero that Arabs resent deeply. In remarkable candor, the interviews explain the critical steps the U.S. government must take before America will once again be revered throughout the region.

— Paul Findley, author of *They Dare to Speak Out: People and Institutions Confront Israel's Lobby*, *Deliberate Deceptions: Facing the Facts About the U.S.-Israeli Relationship*, and *Silent No More: Confronting America's False Images of Islam*

Arab Voices

speak to
American Hearts

by

Samar Dahmash-Jarrah

Edited by Kirt M. Dressler

Arab Voices Speak to American Hearts

Published by   Olive Branch Books
                12776 Westwood Lakes Blvd
                Tampa, FL 33626

ISBN: 0-9769100-8-X

FIRST EDITION, May 2005

Book edited and designed by:

Kirt M. Dressler and the staff of
Superior Writing Services,
1511-R East Fowler Avenue, Suite R
Tampa, Florida, 33612
(813) 972-0159 or toll-free (800) 719-1619
www.superiorwriting.com

Book available at:
www.ArabVoicesSpeak.com

Speaker—The author is available for speaking engagements. Please contact her through the book website

Dedication

This book is dedicated to my late father

Hashem Dahmash,

*who first introduced me to all
that is good in America,
and to my mother*

Soad,

who made it all happen.

Acknowledgements

The hundreds of Americans who attended my classes and lectures in the past fifteen years made this book possible. They made me believe in myself as an ambassador of goodwill between Arabs and Americans. Some of my students encouraged me to write to newspapers and tell the Arab and Muslim side of the story. From them I realized that voices were needed to dispel stereotypes and misinformation about Arab issues—the long-standing Palestinian-Israeli conflict, the September 11th tragedy, the Iraq War, and the U.S. media's one-sided portrayal of Arabs and Islam.

Some of my students were so persistent that one reason I finally decided to write the book was to get some peace! Seriously, you were all very inspiring, but too numerous to list here. I owe my inspiration for this book to your kind prodding, and I thank you all.

Special thanks go to Dr. Hussam Jarrah, Dr. Lama Arabi and Hani Arabi, Ms. Saeda Nour, and Deena Shawwa for believing in my project and for all the help they offered while I conducted interviews in Amman, Jordan. I thank Hooda Shawwa and Dr. Nabil Qaddumi in Kuwait and Dina Dahmash, Ziad Ali, Hashem Ali, and Faiqa Zaki in Cairo, Egypt. They all helped me find candidates for the book's interviews.

My immediate and extended family has been a great support to me. I thank Muhamad Jarrah for the difficult task of translating the interviews conducted in Arabic. His tireless efforts to do this in such a short time are much appreciated and I cherish his assistance.

My young assistant Leslie Wier did a superb job compiling the questions, sorting them, printing them, and preparing them on easy-to-use flash cards. Leslie later worked very hard transcribing those interviews that were conducted in English. Leslie is a young bright spirit who felt that my project was a learning experience for her and I hope that she will continue to work with me.

My editor Kirt Dressler is also a mentor whom I met many years ago while obtaining my Master's degree at the University of

South Florida in Tampa. Kirt changed my life in many positive ways when he exposed me to alternative media and to another face of America that I had not known existed. He enriched my mind and character in ways that I had not imagined possible. He believed in me during those times when my faith in myself was low. He unmercifully criticized me when I "did not have my heart" in the work I was "asking him to edit," as he liked to tell me. I owe my political awareness and some of my love for peaceful coexistence to Kirt. I owe him more than he will ever know.

I would like to thank Mandy Minor and Justin Elza who worked as assistant editors on the book and Sherry Lucciola for typing. Thanks also to my friend Sushila Cherian for all her support throughout the years. She has been a great critic and a great source of advice and comfort. I also thank Dr. Ahmed and Malak Elrefai, Hasan and Barbra Hammami, Kathryn Lyden, and James Abraham for reviewing the manuscript and for their much-needed input.

My gratitude also goes to my mother, who also urged me to write a book and who contributed to the title and cover of the book. She is and will always be Priceless.

Most importantly, since we married fifteen years ago, my husband Mamoon has nagged me as much as my students to use my talents. He has always pushed me to excel and to seek the "higher ground" of what is right and good in life. He is not a typical husband by any means! He is a mentor and a motivator and one book will not satisfy him. He is and will always be *hayati*—my life.

Samar Dahmash-Jarrah,
Port Charlotte, Florida
April, 2005

Table of Contents

continued...

Table of Contents
(continued)

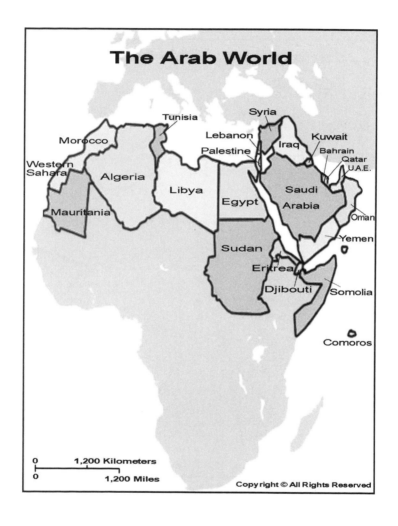

The Arab World

Learning About the Arab World

To better understand the history of the Arab world and the political issues of the region it would be helpful to read more about these issues. Many books explain the modern history of the Arab world—the history of the past two centuries. One such is *A Peace to End All Peace: The Fall of the Ottoman Empire and the Creation of the Modern Middle East* by David Fromkin. This book explains how European influence in the area created false boundaries and artificial borders that are even now a cause for turmoil in the Arab world.

Specifically, both England and France promised Arab independence, then betrayed Arab trust by secretly signing the Sykes-Picot Agreement of May 16, 1916, which divided the Arab world between them. This secret agreement ignored years of correspondence between Sharif Hussein of Mecca and Sir Henry McMahon, British high commissioner in Egypt, which promised Arab independence in exchange for an Arab revolt against the Ottoman Empire.

As if this was not enough to cause Arab anger and mistrust, the League of Nations, Britain, and Zionists conspired to destroy the historical, national, and legal rights of Palestine. Britain had no authority over Palestine, yet promised the country to European Jews, most of whom had never even been there. A detailed account of this can be found in *Bible and Sword* by Barbara W. Tuchman, which chronicles the events that led to that fateful promise on November 2, 1917. On that day British Foreign Secretary Arthur Balfour sent a letter to Baron Rothschild pledging British support for the establishment of a Jewish national home in Palestine, ignoring the fact that Jews made up less than ten percent of Palestine's total population.

To truly understand modern politics in the Arab world, one must learn more about Arab history through the eyes of Arabs and credible authors who do not seek to tarnish or falsify history. The history of Arabs did not start with the Prophet Muhammad (peace be upon him) and Islam fourteen centuries ago; the history of Palestine did not start only 2,000 years ago.

It is also essential that we understand the importance and impact of historical and current foreign intervention in Arab affairs. And it is most important that we know that monotheism originated in the Arab region, thus separating the current religious climate from this history is an inconsistency.

It can be hard for Americans to get an Arab perspective on the Arab world, since most current articles and books on this subject are written in Arabic and not available in English. Thankfully, many English language books have been written about the Palestine problem by authors such as the late Christian Arab Edward Said, whose prolific writing ranged from Arabic thought and scholarship to media coverage of the Arab world. I recommend his books, as well as those of Walid Khalidi.

To understand the daily suffering of Palestinians living under occupation, read Israeli author Amira Hass and American Jewish author Wendy Pearlman (*Occupied Voices: Stories of Everyday Life from the Second Intifada*). To learn more about Islam, read authors such as John Esposito, Michel Wolf, Khaled Abou El Fadl, and Karen Armstrong. The Internet also offers many resources dedicated to Arabs and Muslims; a list of these resources can be found at the back of the book.

How This Book Came About

The idea for this book started many years ago, but became especially persistent a few months after the tragedy of September 11th.   Soon after that horrible event took place on that black Tuesday morning, I found myself thrown into the limelight by requests to speak to Americans about the Arab world and Islam. Less than a week after that fateful day, and after getting tired of watching American television and non-Arab and non-Muslim pundits babbling about how Arabs and Muslims think, many Americans felt that they needed to talk directly to people from that part of the world.

It all started when the local newspaper printed a long feature article on Islam and Arabs and I answered many questions posed by the reporter. This article was published shortly after September 11th and on a Sunday, the highest circulation day of the paper.   Calls for me to speak at local clubs, churches, and synagogues immediately poured in—sometimes I had three or four speaking engagements a week.   Each engagement required preparation and was exhaustive both mentally and physically. I vividly remember the first time I faced the public at a Unitarian Fellowship in Port Charlotte in the presence of local media. I was literally petrified. I could not eat or drink or relax before the event. The only calming factor was the idea that soon it would be over. I thought only of how relieved I would feel after the event.

I did not know how Americans would react to my presence. I was also afraid of the media. I thought, now my face and name will be in front of people who are angry with Muslims and Arabs. What if they lash out in anger at my family and me?

I did not accept these opportunities to speak in order to apologize—I had done nothing. I just wanted Americans to know that Arabs and Muslims were regular people just like them.   I wanted them to know that a democracy should not collapse because of an event like that of September 11th, 2001. America should not abandon its civil liberties and all that its founders struggled to create. Still, I felt deeply uncertain of how audiences would react to me. I am not sure how I managed to speak at all—but it seems that my anxiety was not obvious to my listeners. People told me that I appeared calm and confident—while I felt petrified.

What always kept me going and encouraged me to continue accepting these strenuous public speaking engagements was the reaction of the audiences. People, some in tears, asked me to keep reaching out to Americans—to help them understand and open their eyes to a different viewpoint. The response to my talks was almost always positive, and whenever audience members disagreed they were always civil and polite. Many people said I should be on national television and radio—as if I had any say in this. Many more asked me to write a book. Book? *What book?* I kept asking myself.

I always tried to be honest and truthful in my answers to questions regarding the Middle East as a region. I felt that I was qualified to do so, not only because I was Arab and Muslim, but also because of my education and life-long interest in politics. Since the age of nine I have read newspapers and watched television news every day. In recent years, the Internet and satellite networks have made it even easier to follow minute-by-minute events occurring all over the world. All I really wanted to do was bring Arabs, Muslims, and Americans closer to each other. Having lived in multiple cultures, I knew that we had so many things in common and that the fault lines were artificial and could easily go away.

As time passed and I had spoken to hundreds of groups, I realized that I was increasingly answering questions on the minds of Americans that were directed at Arabs living in the Arab world. Americans were not only asking political questions, they were also posing basic questions about the average Arab, questions related to their daily lives and impressions of Americans. In other words, I was answering on behalf of Arabs still living in the Arab world, yet I had become an Arab-American and no longer lived there!

In addition, being an Arab-American is not a cliché or just a definition to make the census easier. It is not just a statistic. The term Arab-American means that I am no longer 100% pure Arab. I am also an American and think and behave in many ways just like an American. Soon I realized that I could no longer speak on behalf of Arabs since it had been three years since I last visited the Arab world. Momentous events had occurred since then— September 11th and two wars! I still monitored news coming from the Arab world on a daily basis, but I felt that three years absence from the region was a long time for me to be able to answer such questions accurately.

The more I spoke to Americans the more I realized that I needed to visit and talk to Arabs. I felt that I needed to see the Arab world again through my own eyes and not through someone else's lens or essay. I had to feel it inside my heart to be able to talk about all walks of life in Arab nations. So I planned my trip to include visits to Jordan, Lebanon, and Egypt. Lebanon was later replaced by Kuwait in order to represent the views of Arabs living in the Gulf countries. Indeed, I had initially envisioned the trip as a family visit, but the more I thought about it, the more I realized that I needed to gather information from Arabs in a systematic way. But I had no clue where to start and how to document what I would see there.

I thought of submitting columns to newspapers that had published my essays in the past, but I needed to reach as many Americans as possible—even those who did not read newspapers. I wanted Arabs and Americans to talk to each other without barriers and borders. I wanted to take all those questions that Americans kept asking me directly to the Arab people and say: "This is what average Americans want to know about you. This is your chance to tell them how you think and feel with no censor or government standing between you and them."

I had planned to leave on Sunday, August 15, 2004, but as my departure date loomed, I still did not know exactly how to approach this project. I was quickly running out of time. But it is amazing how good ideas often occur while you are far from home and miles away from paper and pencil. The idea hit me while sweating and speeding beyond my ability on a fifty-mile bicycle ride with extremely fit people. Out of breath and energy, the solution suddenly hit me. *Why don't I just e-mail Americans and ask them this:* "If you had a chance to ask an Arab a question, what would it be?" I literally saw the cliché idea "light-bulb" (it was only the Florida August sun) and rushed home to write an e-mail.

I sent the e-mail to every American I knew and asked them to send it to everyone they knew and so on. The response was overwhelming. As e-mails jammed my inbox, I could clearly see that I had something solid in my hands—no longer just an idea. My amorphous project had suddenly taken shape. Indeed, I could not keep up with the deluge of e-mails and the encouraging messages of support from people I had never met in my life who liked the idea of posing their questions directly to Arabs. The response came more like a chain letter reaction; I received e-mails from college students, recent graduates, lawyers, peace activists, hard-core conservatives, journalists, business professionals, army veterans, and grandmothers.

Then my trip was delayed suddenly by Hurricane Charlie, and I started to get bogged down in the clean-up and every day struggle after this natural disaster while the e-mails kept coming. The questions piled up and the whole idea of writing a book became a burden to me. I felt that the task ahead was larger than me—all I wanted from this trip was to see family and friends and get a feel for the Arab world while enjoying hummus, kebab, and shisha!

One other concern filled my mind—I had not told my family members in the three countries that I was coming to write a book. They were already upset that I had ruined their summer plans with the four-week delay in my trip, so I did not expect them to appreciate the book idea at all. I even thought that any Arab I met would ridicule the idea of my book. Why should they care to answer questions on the minds of Americans? Maybe they really did not like Americans and did not care much for what Americans thought.

My dear friend Hooda, whom I have known since college days in Cairo, called to check on me after watching Charlie wipe out Punta Gorda and Port Charlotte live on TV. Suddenly I wondered if Hooda could be my "test balloon" and told her about my idea for the book. To my amazement and shock she absolutely loved it and immediately supported me. She even offered to accompany me to any country I intended to visit and suggested I include Kuwait. She told me: "We Arabs need to be talking directly to Americans. Americans cannot come to us, so why not go to them through your book?" This positive reaction comforted me and there was no turning back after that.

My young assistant Leslie put all the questions on flash cards and, after eliminating the repetitive ones, we ended up with 100 cards, each containing a different question. The task ahead of me would begin as soon as I set foot in Amman, Jordan. The persistent questions on my mind were: "Who on earth am I going to ask these questions to? How will I find candidates for such questions?" The answer turned out to be very simple—I would ask people similar to those who asked the questions in the first place!

I also decided to include Christian Arabs (three of the twelve interviewees) to show the diversity of the Arab world. Furthermore, another commonality between Arabs and Americans was revealed in that six of the twelve interviewees conducted their interviews in English, as they knew English very well.

The Americans who sent me their questions were middle class, from all sorts of professions, and a few were retired. I decided not to interview anyone who currently worked for any government department or institution. I also decided I would not interview friends or relatives, only total strangers. Thus started my journey—one that had actually begun fifteen years before when I moved to the U.S.

This move from the Arab world was a turning point in my life, a life I had spent as a stateless Palestinian moving with my family from one country to another, always seeking a home. All told I lived in five countries before coming to the U.S. My brothers and sisters and I were all born in Kuwait, and I later lived in Lebanon, Saudi Arabia, Egypt, and Jordan. The interviews in this book are the fruit of that journey. Enjoy!

My Remarkable Subjects

The twelve Arab men and women interviewed in this book never hesitated to talk about tough issues. They never let concerns for their own safety keep them from voicing criticism about their societies, religious establishments, or governments. In turn, I felt obligated to present their words with a minimum of editing. None of them asked me not to reveal their names, although I chose to include only first names to maintain simplicity and spark curiosity.

When I embarked on this project, I worried that it would be a total failure. I feared people in the Arab world would not trust that I was just an ordinary person who wanted their voices to be heard in America. I thought they would meet me with suspicion and assume that I worked for some American intelligence agency. But only one interviewee bluntly asked me about this—and, even then, not until after we had finished the interview.

Still, I did not expect people to open up so easily to a total stranger. People in the Arab world are not used to being asked their opinions about important issues like religion, politics, democracy, and war. So I was amazed at the frankness of the twelve respondents and, at times, the courage they displayed in speaking their minds.

I felt most surprised by the unbelievable degree of enthusiasm everyone I interviewed had for the project itself. It often felt as if they were suffocating, gasping for air—and my tape recorder helped them to breathe. Those interviewed—and the many others who are not in this book, but knew about it—felt an urgent need to talk directly to Americans, person-to-person. Although Americans have shown keen interest in the project as well, it seemed that the Arabs I met had a much greater sense of urgency about communicating.

Writing this book was a continuous learning experience, one that forced me to do quite a bit of soul-searching. While interviewing my twelve subjects, I noticed that my thoughts constantly shifted from East to West and West to East, as I tried to imagine how both Americans and Arabs would react to the Arab interviewees' responses to questions posed by Americans.   I sometimes found myself fascinated by the thoughts and ideas revealed to me; I often could not believe that an Arab would actually say such things.   I felt both amazed and thrilled at the frankness, intellectual sophistication, and emotional involvement that my subjects conveyed on a variety of topics.

Some of the interviewees' comments are critical, and others may even sound a bit harsh, but these are the kinds of thoughts that are on people's minds in the Arab world.   When I began the process of compiling, translating, and editing the interview transcripts, I found myself questioning whether I should delete certain words or sentences that might seem offensive to some. After much agonizing, I concluded that we understand each other better when we are honest about our feelings.

When people go to counseling they spell out all that is bothering and hurting them and, through this brutal honesty, the healing process can begin.   Therefore, I decided to leave the interviews "as is"—whether positive, negative, "good," "bad," inspiring, or depressing.   I wanted to let the reader go through a soul searching trip, too.   Thus, the editing primarily focused on eliminating repetition and clarifying meaning.

As a critic of media bias and censorship, I would be a hypocrite if I removed words like "racist," "fascist," "fanatic," "retarded,"   "crazy,"   or "maniac" from the text.   The whole adventure of this book was introducing people in the United States and elsewhere to how Arabs think.   If I removed such words, I would have betrayed the very essence of my project, and more importantly, my own soul.   I would also have betrayed my twelve subjects.

The people I interviewed in each of the three countries were chosen as randomly as possible.   Most of the time, I went with my gut feeling when referred to possible interviewees.   As mentioned earlier, I never knew any of them before the interviews, and none were relatives, acquaintances, friends, or had any official or governmental capacity.   These were all conditions that I made sure were maintained, although it meant that many good candidates were left out.

As it turned out, in many ways my twelve Arab subjects mirrored the variety of Americans who posed the questions— lawyers, pastors, radio hosts, journalists, conservatives, humanists, students, and grandmothers sent me their questions and their counterparts in the Arab world responded. Serendipity.

I would like to remind readers that the opinions herein belong solely to the people interviewed. I do not necessarily agree with everything they said. At times, some of the comments opposed my own views, but the only honest approach for me was to separate myself from the subjects and their opinions. The true test of democracy, in my opinion, is to be able to live as an individual. Not tampering with what people say is how I try to accomplish this.

Arab Voices
speak to American Hearts

Interviews

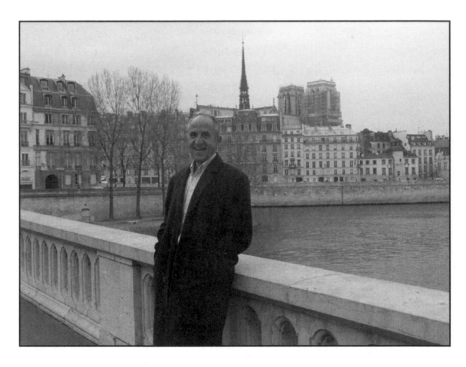

Mohamed on vacation in Paris

Mohamed, 58
Business Executive
Cairo, Egypt
Muslim

As individuals, Americans are nice people, and are still considered by our people to be nice people. When you meet Americans and talk to them you find that they're warm, generous, have fantastic qualities, rarely lie, have excellent management skills, and are very open and straightforward. As individuals, they have wonderful qualities, but as politicians and as a government, they're as low as one can get.

Introduction

I met Mohamed in a high-rise Cairo office building overlooking the Nile in an area called al Maadi where many foreign expatriates reside. My early morning drive took me through narrow one-way streets filled with Egyptians struggling against heavy traffic to reach their destinations. Students and patients headed to the old al Qaser al Eini Hospital in Cairo, a teaching hospital that treats patients free of charge. Horse- and mule-drawn carriages competed with pedestrians, cars, and busses for space in the narrow streets bordering the Nile.

On the opposite side of the street stood old buildings with impressive architecture; some looked Islamic while others appeared French or Roman. Some seemed to have been palaces once inhabited by the rich that now functioned as schools and

3

government offices. An amazing mix of history and nature made me nostalgic as I drove on.

The Nile is unlike any river I have ever seen. Mysterious and powerful, it looks like a stream of thick olive oil. It narrows in some places and widens in others, with lush green islands in the middle. It is easy to close your eyes and imagine the days of ancient Egypt, when each year a young girl was "wedded" to the Nile in hopes that this would please the river and no flood would come that year.

Mamluks on horseback, Napoleon Bonaparte and his French wine in the middle of Arabia, Lord Kitchener and his invading armies marching into the Sudan—every street corner in Egypt speaks volumes of these and other historical events. I closed my eyes and tried to imagine how many books I would need to write just to explain Egypt and Egyptians to Americans. There is so much history, language, and culture in Egypt to be explored; so much antiquity in the air waiting to be inhaled.

Meet Mohamed

I was born and raised in Cairo, Egypt and educated at a French Catholic school. I come from a middle class family; my father was a government employee and owned a small parcel of agricultural property he inherited from my grandparents. I have worked for IBM for many years in Egypt, Saudi Arabia, and the company's European headquarters in France, where I was responsible for the Middle East and part of Africa. After that I worked as a management consultant, and now work at a telecom company in Egypt.

I speak Arabic, English, and French fluently. I've traveled to many places in the world and I have many interests in life. I am married and three of my children work abroad. One son is a cardiac surgeon in Canada, another is a lawyer on assignment in Paris for his New York law firm, and the third works for an

American company in Dubai. I also have one daughter, who studied psychology and lives with us here in Cairo.

I consider myself to be reasonably rational and educated. I was fortunate enough to have a unique French education. Most of my teachers, whom I greatly respect and admire, were monks. Not quite priests, but people who devoted their lives to educating children. Their rational thinking influenced the way I analyze issues and problems.

At the school they taught Arabic, English, and French. Most of the professors were French nationals, but the school itself was not a French government school. The student body was extremely cosmopolitan; we had Lebanese, Yugoslav, Italian, French, German, and Spanish students. These students brought with them a variety of religious backgrounds and denominations— Catholic, Mennonite, Orthodox, Protestant, Jewish, and Muslim students all learned together. A person's nationality was not discussed; for us, it was "business as usual" when it came to living in an environment with kids from different backgrounds.

We spoke different languages at home, but at school we spoke French. Some parents were more permissive, allowing their daughters to go to dances, while others were more conservative. We saw this diversity as simply a fact of life and did not place value judgments. I think I was very lucky to grow up in such an ethnically diverse environment.

After high school I first attended the University of Cairo to study engineering and later received an MBA from the American University in Cairo (AUC). I worked for many years before deciding to go back to school to obtain a Master's degree in Islamic Art and Architecture from AUC. I decided to study this while living in France; almost every cab driver in Paris knew the history of their old buildings. In Egypt we study the pyramids and the Sphinx, but ironically little about the history of Islamic monuments. I was embarrassed when colleagues asked me about buildings in Cairo and I had no clue what they were talking about. I felt ashamed that Parisian cab drivers knew so much about their country but I, an engineer with an MBA, knew so little about Cairo.

To remedy this, I took a class called Art and Architecture of the City of Cairo. It so fascinated me that I decided to earn an architecture degree. Learning about Cairo was so marvelous that I decided to travel to all sorts of places with interesting architecture. I visited India, Pakistan, Spain, Turkey, Tunis, Syria, and Morocco to photograph monuments. My photos are not professional and I would never think of publishing them in a book, but I enjoyed taking them and cherish the memories.

*   *   *

There are religious fundamentalists everywhere in the world—in Egypt, the United States, Canada, France—and the actions of extremists are reported in the news more than others. I think that religious fundamentalists have so much power over the rest of the Arab world because extremists in general have more visibility. You might not report that a man went to work, but you would report that somebody punched someone else in the face. Those who do extreme things are mentioned more often in the news; people who go to work every day and are good citizens are not.

Look at Timothy McVeigh or David Korresh in the U.S. There are millions of other men who have never done such extreme things, but you only hear about the extremists. Reporting that only covers extremists makes one think the whole world is full of extremists, or in the case of Arabs and Muslims, as if all of us are extremists.

I believe the cause of the current wave of terrorism is the Palestinian problem. People in the Arab world are greatly frustrated because of what is happening to the Palestinians on a daily basis. It is not an issue that happened a long time ago and is now over with; it is an ongoing problem and we see it every day on TV. We see the injustice inflicted on the Palestinians with our own eyes. Palestinians are being killed every day in a "free-for-all," but how much of this gets on American TV news? Almost none. When an Israeli is killed it is all over the news. But we Arabs see the Palestinian struggle on TV every day, we read about it, and it makes us sad, upset, and frustrated.

I remember reading in a leading American newspaper many years ago about a group of Israelis who were hiking in the Palestinian occupied territories when they saw a flashlight in the dark and shot at it. They assumed that the light was coming from a Palestinian terrorist when it was really a young Israeli girl. Her tragic death was a major headline, but buried in the same paper was only a few lines about three Palestinian civilians killed on the same day by Israeli occupation forces. Can you believe that I still remember the name of that young Israeli girl? She was Hilda Polat, and I still feel sad for her parents who lost their daughter in this way. Hilda's was only one of four lives lost that day, but only she warranted headline coverage. Why?

This double standard in measuring the loss of life causes much resentment in the Arab world. Add to this all the Security Council resolutions on the question of Palestine that were never implemented and all the vetoes by the U.S. government against any attempt to condemn Israeli violence, and you have a formula for anger and frustration that makes people want to get back at the American government. But how? This is where extremists enter the picture, trying to deal with their political frustrations through violent means. So, as long as U.S. policy towards the Palestinians is seen as unjust and not even-handed, Arab people will be angry at the U.S.

But we as Arab countries are also to blame, because we are not well organized and have a lot of deficiencies. We don't know how to work together—we're not united, which adds to the people's frustration. If our countries were united and better organized, we would probably have less extremism. But as long as there is a Palestinian problem, there will be a reason for people to be extremists.

Most anger is directed at the American government and not the American people themselves. Even during the worst days of

our relations with America, no American had any problems
walking in the streets of Cairo, being welcomed in our homes, or
going to clubs. I remember going to a nightclub where the show
director asked, "Anyone from France?" People in the audience
would say yes and Egyptians cheered. Then he asked, "Anyone
from America?" And someone in the audience said yes and
Egyptians cheered. This was soon after the 1967 War when we
were being crushed by the U.S., but still Americans were never
hated in Egypt.

I think we have more political awareness than the average
American because we live a daily tragedy with Palestine, and we
are more exposed to national and international politics and world
events than Americans. Today there is an additional tragedy Arabs
are facing: the Iraq War. We feel that America is focusing all its
power on Arabs and Muslims. The American government is
talking about Syria, Iran, and Darfur all the time, as though nothing
else is going on in the rest of the world. Why don't you go to
Zimbabwe and South America and see what lousy things are
happening there? But the U.S. government and media focus only
on Arab and Muslim countries and nothing else. We get blow after
blow either in the form of a veto or more weapons sold to Israel or
news of Israelis helping Americans interrogate prisoners in Abu
Ghraib prison in Iraq. Political awareness makes us stay current on
what is going on and it hurts us to know. Americans do not know
what is really going on, but they should. They need to know what
their government is doing in their name and try to correct this
destructive path.

Solving the Palestinian problem will make it harder for
extremists to exist. However, extremists everywhere—Egypt,
Argentina, Peru, etc.—will continue to exist; only the target of
their anger will change. Their target will no longer be the U.S., but
their own governments or their neighbors or their cousins or the
woman who's not veiled or the man who is doing something they
don't like.

There are extremists everywhere. Look at the skinheads [neo-Nazis] in Germany. Why isn't Russia the target of their anger? Because they have nothing against Russia. They are angry at immigrants to Germany, and Russia has nothing to do with this. Similarly, Egyptian extremists are mad at American foreign policy, so they try to hurt America to force America's policies to change.

I think that the war in Iraq has caused more extremism, because it is based on lies that everyone knows are lies. Bush is an extremist; he is someone who does not use logic. For him, it's black or white. There are no shades of gray; you are either with us or against us. He does not think in terms of compromise. He is convinced that he is right and everyone else has to accept it or face the consequences. I think that he is really a religious fundamentalist, just like many other world leaders.

Saddam was bad, but he is not the only bad leader out there. There are many in Latin America, Africa, Korea, China— the list goes on. Is China a democracy that does not imprison and torture people? Of course not—look at the Tibetan occupation! So why doesn't Bush remove the Chinese leaders from power since they are doing essentially the same thing as Saddam? Why only Saddam?

The war against Iraq had nothing to do with weapons of mass destruction. There are many forces behind this war, and one major one is the neo-conservatives. They have been pushing to invade Iraq since 1992 and are the very ones who, according to Plan of Attack by Bob Woodward, went to see Bush right after September 11th and urged him to invade Iraq.

Why the rush to invade Iraq? Major powers should find out what happened first, and then if there is still reason to think Iraq had something to do with September 11th, then invade—but not before.

In my mind the neo-cons are also very pro-Israel, because they are a part of the very pro-Israel Likud think tanks with Feith, Wolfowitz, and Richard Perle. These people pushed to invade Iraq because they thought that eliminating Saddam and his army would neutralize any possible credible force in the Arab world. They are simply acting with the safety of Israel in mind, not the safety of America.

The "icing on the cake" is oil and control of a world economy that depends on oil. And revenge also. Bush once said of Saddam, "he is the man who tried to kill my dad." So, maybe Bush is also acting out of revenge. But the real reason behind the war is a president who wants to be reelected at any cost looking at his constituents and thinking that helping Israel's security will please them and win him reelection.

How can this type of thing happen in a democracy? Because most of the 300 million people in America form their opinions from news reports that are decidedly pro-Israel. The newspapers, TV stations, and magazines have pro-Israel writers and reporters who know how to express things very well in sound bytes that are easily understood and accepted by the general public.

This is not a conspiracy theory; it is just a reality that many Americans in positions of media power are emotionally connected to Israel. Rupert Murdoch of FOX news is staunchly pro-Likud Israel and his TV station is where many Americans get their information and news.

The film documentary *Control Room* was created by two young women, one Lebanese-American and one Egyptian-American, who were in Qatar during the invasion of Iraq. Their film is about the way the media reported the war, showing the censorship and self-censorship by American reporters and journalists. They also show how the U.S. Army and defense establishment manipulates things to show American soldiers as happy, successful, attractive, and that everything was going according to plan while at the same time showing all Iraqis as ugly and almost inhuman.

This is why the American government hated al Jazeera— because it showed the other side of the story. It showed the suffering of the people, the innocent civilian deaths, and the ugliness of war and its human toll. This is a part of the war that Americans never got a chance to see, so they ended up being manipulated by both government and media. Americans did not even see their own body bags. But had they seen them and the suffering of the Iraqi people, the destruction, the misery and the horrid things associated with war, Americans would start asking tough questions. They would say, we have created all this misery and this entire terrible situation—for what? But thanks to media bias, most Americans think that everything is perfect. It doesn't even matter why America went to war with Iraq or if it was justified. For Americans, life goes on; for us, misery goes on.

*   *   *

I feel that the Abu Ghraib prison scandal added to the hypocrisy of the U.S. government's discourse on democracy and moral values. We all know that the U.S. government says things publicly and does the opposite secretly. But with Abu Ghraib we have pictures—we have evidence of this hypocrisy. The Abu Ghraib scandal was just unbelievable. It's not like an interrogation where somebody says "He's not giving us any information, so he's of no use" and then punches him in the nose. It's far more sinister—it's people having bloody fun humiliating others. We don't do this in our prisons, but we're supposed to be the backward country! Yes, we mistreat prisoners—but never for fun.

I think the soldiers who did these horrible things in the prison were brainwashed to think Iraqi prisoners are cockroaches. So it was easy to torture them; it was like killing a cockroach. No one who has killed a cockroach before hesitates to do it again. I think the U.S. soldiers had very little respect, understanding, or empathy towards the Iraqi prisoners, and that attitude is something that comes from the top down. It's not necessarily a direct order to attach a leash to a prisoner. It's a style, an attitude, a culture among those in charge who look down at Iraqis and their culture, and this filters from the top to the bottom ranks.

It is the culture and style of people like army generals, elected officials, and even President Bush to say "Bring 'em on." What kind of language and attitude is this? This is child's talk, child's play! This isn't baseball; this is war where real lives are at stake. This style makes the American soldiers on the ground behave this way and think it is acceptable—because it is to American leaders.

I tried to find some rationalization for the soldiers' behavior, but I could not. The soldiers were having fun with the lives of other people, with the humanity of other people. And I do not think that this abuse stopped at the Abu Ghraib prison. I read about private prisons in Afghanistan where a general was being interrogated and they killed him in the process. What happened in Iraq took away the fig leaf of moral superiority of the American way of life—as a government and as policies.

*   *   *

As individuals, Americans are nice people, and are still considered by our people to be nice people. When you meet Americans and talk to them you find that they're human, generous, have fantastic qualities, rarely lie, have excellent management skills, and are very open and straightforward. As individuals, they have wonderful qualities, but as politicians and a government, they're as low as one can get.

What I especially don't like about America is the manipulation of the press. If you don't know what I'm talking about take a look at British or German or Russian newspapers. You'll always find more balance than you see in U.S. papers.

As for President Bush, I don't think he's educated or cultured. I don't think he has traveled enough in the world, or talked to enough people from different cultures and different parts of the world. He actually boasts that he does not read books or newspapers! I think he's limited in his mental abilities and when you're limited you want simple things around you so that you can understand and control them. And that's why he sees people as right or wrong, black or white, with me or against me. He doesn't have the mental ability of Clinton or other previous American presidents. He's too simplistic and he is not much help when it comes to having better relations with the rest of the world. He says we hate democracy and hate America, but he is wrong.

There was a survey in Arab countries that showed most Arabs surveyed hated American *policies*. However, they did not say that they hated Canada or Canada's democracy. The Arabs did not say they hated democracy or hated Canada because it is a democratic country. They said they hated U.S. policies, the U.S. government, Bush, Cheney. They don't hate individual Americans or the West in general or democracy. They actually admire the democracies of Canada, Sweden, Britain, and Germany. But they do hate Bush and Cheney and the neo-cons.

I am not sure if things will be different if Kerry is elected president. All politicians are interested in getting reelected and so tend to cater to whoever finances their political campaigns—and we all know that pro-Israeli groups are more powerful than pro-Arab groups. I want the American government to be more even-handed, to listen more, and listen with empathy. I want the American government and politicians to have more balanced views and actions in the Middle East. It is in America's best interest to work with the Middle East on an equal footing. It is also in the best interest of Middle Eastern governments to become more serious and more democratic.

If you had asked me ten years ago what the Arab world needed I would *not* have said democracy. We needed an enlightened and strong leader who could have improved our economy and got the country back on the right economic track. But now we need democracy—not necessarily a British, German, or Italian form of democracy, but one where people participate in the decision-making and the election of new governments, so that the government doesn't become complacent or corrupt. We need a democracy where if I, as a citizen, am not pleased with the government's policies, then I can change it through elections. I might not be happy with the new government that I just elected, but it doesn't matter. I have participated in elections and maybe next time I will elect a better government. The process itself will make me feel that I have a stake in my country.

Democracy is very specific for me. It must have a very free press where the ills of government can be exposed. There also must be teamwork, maybe within a multi-party system, where several teams work together within a party to develop a program for the country. Then eventually when a particular party is elected, it brings to government a team that has worked together for five or ten years where members know each other and know how to work well together and can get things done.

Today when we form a government, we bring in nice people who are from different places and hope for the best. This is not the way to run a country; this is not even the way to run a grocery store! But if you have a team that is harmonious and was elected by the people because of its political and economic plan, the team members will be tougher in their decision-making because they have legitimacy. Our governments are so scared of doing anything that is unpopular (like lifting some food subsidies) that they just let things go on, which leads to political and economic disaster. Democracy is necessary for the long-term welfare of the country. Perhaps in a few years we will be using the same terminology that other people who live in democratic systems use, or maybe we will say we have taken our country back and are shaping it according to how we think it should look in the future.

I think we missed an opportunity in Egypt to change. President Mubarak has been in power now for more than twenty years, and I think that after his first few years in power he could have encouraged the other parties to participate in the governance of the country. He should have done that. He should have encouraged the drive for freedom of the press. Now it is a bit late for him to start all this. Probably the younger leaders in other countries like Morocco can do things like this, but I do not see change happening in Egypt because we have to think of the transition if something happens to Mubarak. We know that the people in power now will not be happy if they lose control, and this is what is on the minds of Egyptians at this time.

I know that the U.S. wants to bring democracy to the Arab world, and I do not mind this. But after the invasion of Iraq anything that comes from the U.S. comes with a bad name. People now have a worse attitude in the Arab world towards the U.S. government than ever before. But we should not reject things simply because they come from the U.S. If we do, we would be accepting the arguments put forth by our governments when they refuse to improve things because changes or improvements are associated with the U.S. I do not mind help from the U.S. or other Western countries like France, Germany, and the U.K., but I don't think change will come from the West. It has to evolve within the Middle East and cannot be dictated to us.

Democracy has to be internalized and desired by people. It's like the Rotary Club; we all have to accept the rules of the game. If you go to the Rotary Club and don't accept the rules you cannot belong. Democracy is similar to this. It's not just a matter of having written in a constitution that you must hold elections, so you hold formal ones. It's a matter of people *believing* in elections and accepting that this is the right way so that they *will* vote. Democracy must be internalized and accepted, and this will come only once people actually participate in the process. We used to have this in Egypt before the revolution in 1952; we had a parliament and parties and votes in Egypt, and we had the function of a democracy. So the question is, can this come back? I believe that it can.

It is going to take time; this is true. It will not be perfect at the beginning, but in ten or fifteen years it will be better, because we have to go through the process of participation and government alternation until we learn the process and accept its practice. Then it will become part of us—a way of life and the norm.

We are a people of differing opinions. Leaders whom I disagree with can come to power, but I will respect the result and the process and I will vote them out the next election. Democracy needs to become part of our cultural tradition. It is not at the moment, but not because as Arabs or Muslims we are inherently undemocratic. If you look at many nations in Africa you will find that they have the same problem, and we cannot explain this by saying they are undemocratic because of their color or geographic location. The same thing is true with China.

Democracy is a matter of building tradition from the bottom up through efforts to encourage multi-party systems, freedom of the press, and free elections. The people need to call on their leaders to do these things and not sit idle and wait for it to happen. It is going to take time, because we don't have the tradition and the majority of people are not asking for change yet.

It is wrong to say that lack of democracy is intrinsic to Islam or Arabs. There are democracies that are working and improving over time in Islamic countries—look at Indonesia, Turkey, and Bangladesh. Many Americans will not accept this example, but it is working in Iran, too.

Our democracy is not going to be a "true democracy" until it becomes the regular thing, because we have to learn it, practice it, accept it. And as we practice, it will become like our DNA and normal. There is nothing in Islam that stops us from being democratic, just as there is nothing in Africa, Burma, or Vietnam to stop people from being democratic. The government systems are to blame, because they do not want to introduce the democratic process; it threatens their existence. It will take the people to change this—not the West and not foreign armies.

*   *   *

I'm not sure if the U.S. is trying to indoctrinate the Arab world. However, if I were the U.S. government I would try to make every country love me. I would try to make all the educational systems in all the countries say that the U.S. is the best country in the world.

If the U.S. government is trying to do this, I can't blame them. If Egypt was very well-organized, it would try to convince all countries that it is the most wonderful country in the world. But for the U.S. to do more than this, like what we read in the media about changing things in the Quran, well, this is stupid. Only an uneducated person would say such a thing! You don't change books of faith—not the New Testament or the Old Testament or the Quran. You can't tell someone not to teach their children religion.

If you look at the texts of the Old Testament you will find extreme things, like the way a man must treat his wife and what happens to her if her husband dies. If one takes things out of context or explains incidents that took place centuries ago, according to today's world one will not do justice to religion. There are words in the holy books that can be interpreted in different ways and affect the meaning, so one should not pick on such things.

If I had an opportunity to ask an American one question it would be, "What would it take for you to be interested in knowing more about us? What can we do to get you to want to know more about us—to visit or read something about our history and culture?" I would like to see Americans interested in a television program about our country—about our problems and aspirations. What will it take for this to happen?

Kamil with his twin daughters in Amman, Jordan

Kamil, 35
Businessman
Amman, Jordan
Christian

We have one paramount problem in the Arab world: the Palestinians. The Arab-Israeli-Palestinian struggle has been going on for 50 years and there is no resolution in sight. The region has endured decades and decades of agony and suffering because of this problem. The Palestinians are the only people in the whole world today who are stateless, and this is unacceptable.

Introduction

Meeting with Kamil was very easy—all I had to do was cross the street from my mom's house. I met Kamil at the Four Seasons in Amman, which opened two years ago. Mom always wondered why someone built such a fancy hotel in Amman. She thought it was built in the hopes that one day foreigners would descend on the city in huge numbers. It turns out she was right, but few thought that in a couple of years there would be so many foreigners descending on Amman. The sad reason was the invasion of Iraq.

Kamil was late but kind enough to call the reception desk and ask them to tell "the woman who looks like she is waiting for someone" that he would be fifteen minutes late. He showed up exactly fifteen minutes later. I was impressed!

Sitting in the shiny art deco hotel lobby brought back memories of my days at Jordan TV, when I used to wait in hotel lobbies for the various VIPs I interviewed or while taking a break from covering a conference or meeting. It is amazing how fate can take a person from one continent to another and, in the end, that person feels part of both. I thought, "Here I am fifteen years later, back to do more reporting, but this time to bring the people of two continents closer together."

Fate is an amazing thing. When Americans ask me how and why I came to the U.S., I have to say, "It was an accident of history."

I remember vividly when I met with James Abourezk, former senator from South Dakota and the founder of the American Arab Anti-Discrimination Committee (ADC), and the late John Halabi, father of Queen Noor, who came to Amman to raise awareness of ADC's mission in the U.S. and to raise funds (Queen Noor grew up as an ordinary Arab-American girl and ended up marrying King Hussein of Jordan, in 1977).

As soon as my interview with Senator Aburezk ended, he handed me his business card and told me to call him if I moved to the U.S.—he wanted me to join his organization. I took the card, smiled at him, and said to myself, "What an amazing thought. He thinks that I can just leave Jordan and move to America and join his ADC!" Little did I know that soon my mom would be plotting with my future husband's cousin to bring the man I would marry all the way from Port Charlotte, Florida to Jordan to meet me. Five years later I was in Washington D.C attending the annual national conference of ADC as an American citizen!

Kamil arrived, interrupting my thoughts and bringing me back to reality.

Meet Kamil

I am Kamil, a 35-year-old Jordanian Arab born in Amman, the capital of Jordan, on August 14, 1969. I spent most of my youth in Amman, but went to the United States at age 18 to complete my BA and MA in economics and political science at Case Western University in Cleveland, Ohio. I returned to Jordan after I finished college and then went back to the United States in

1998 for two years at Kellogg Northwestern University in Chicago, where I earned an MBA. I was married two years ago and have twin girls, Zain and Leena. We just celebrated their first birthday two days ago.

Many Americans wonder if Arabs have heard of Jesus Christ. Absolutely. I am a Christian Arab and my family is descended from this part of the world—we have been in the Arab world for hundreds and hundreds of years. It so happens that Jesus Christ was baptized forty-five minutes away from my home in Amman, Jordan. We are the cradle of Christianity, where Christianity began. Palestine and parts of Jordan are considered "The Holy Land." Christianity is very much embedded in our thoughts, in our upbringing, in our education, and in our way of life.

Under the Jordanian constitution we are all considered Jordanians, irrespective of our religion or belief system. We are treated equally under the constitution and this is how I feel as a Christian Jordanian.

I am proud to say that Christians in Jordan form about six percent of the total population. If you drove around Amman you would be shocked at the number of Christian churches and the peaceful coexistence between Muslims and Christians and between the various Christian denominations within Jordan. I think this has a lot to do with our late King Hussein, who strove to create equality amongst Jordanians irrespective of their ethnicity, religion, or political affiliation. We have the freedom to celebrate our religious holidays very vocally and openly. Our Muslim friends visit with us during Christmas and Easter, and we join them in celebrating their holidays and religious festivities.

I attended first grade at a French school with branches throughout the Arab world. Our teachers were a group of French brothers who dedicated their lives to teaching students French methodology and Christian tradition. Even though the school was a Christian school, when they started teaching religion they separated me from my Muslim friends. We went to a certain class for our Christian religion classes and our Muslim friends went to another class. That was the first time I became aware that there were differences between the religions.

There are three main monotheistic religions: Judaism, Christianity, and Islam. I started learning about these religions while still very young, and as the years passed I began to feel more and more that all were equal. We are all the children of God; he sent his envoys to carry his message, and we have to respect and accept these religions "as is" and deal with them accordingly. In the end, humanity has no particular religious identity and this is a belief that we grew up with here. I am very proud to say that my best friends are Muslims and I see no difference whatsoever between us. I used to fast during the month of Ramadan with my Muslim friends when we were young and break the fasting with them in their houses.

None of us tried to influence each other's religious beliefs. All we cared about was being together during religious festivities—we celebrated so many! Something that is very important for Westerners to understand is that there are advocates of Islam and Christian missionaries everywhere who have dedicated their lives to trying to convert people to their religion. This is their prerogative, and you have to respect them. If people choose to listen to them, that is their decision. But people in the West do not know that there is no compulsion in Islam. Muslims believe that no one can force people to change their religion, and this is something that I've experienced with my Muslim friends all my life.

*   *   *

"Democracy" is a word that is used very loosely today. I very much believe in democracy and the freedom of choice. I believe in a country that respects the rule of law, a country that creates a sense of civic duty and responsibility for its citizens. It's important for people to understand what civic duties are, because it's not just what the country has to offer you, but also what you as a citizen have to offer your country in return.

Historically speaking, some democracies have come at a very heavy cost. Let's look at the U.S. as a model. Democracy came to America at a heavy price—a colonial period of occupation, a revolution, and a Civil War that caused widespread damage and destruction. Democracy doesn't just happen; it takes a long time and the costs are high.

I think that before you can have a political democracy you need to have an economic democracy. Before somebody can vote, he has to be able to pay his bills and feed his family. Economic prosperity and economic democracy are preludes to real political democracy, and this is the case in probably half of the Arab world today. In Jordan we have a benevolent monarchy, and we are lucky to have it. Despite the fact that I grew up under martial law I've never felt that I lived in a dictatorship, in the kind of environment where if you spoke out against the government you would be taken to jail. We've never lived in such an environment.

I believe that the modern form of Western democracy won't necessarily work in this part of the world. We have to take a lot of steps before we can attain such a level of democracy. Iraq is an example—a scary example for me, because there is such diversity in ethnicity and religious identity. Even within each religious identity you have many denominations, each of which is struggling to obtain a piece of the political pie. So Iraqis and whoever is in charge need to be careful about how that pie is divided and who the stakeholders are. They have to create a vested interest for all Iraqis to participate in the new political life in Iraq and make all Iraqis rise above each group's ethnic identity and believe in something larger and more noble than their individual interests. They need Iraqis to believe in a collective interest for the majority.

I believe some form of democracy applies in the Middle East and should apply here. To me democracy is very valuable. Look at the rich democratic West with its strong economy, enabling it to deal with all sorts of problems. It can easily proclaim that its democracy is the best in the world, but is it really? Look at the USA PATRIOT Act in the U.S., which allows the federal government to strip a citizen of his citizenship because some of the money he donated ended up in the hands of what they define as a terrorist organization. This is democracy at its worst.

*   *   *

For me, September 11th is still a mystery. I was shocked at the news and believe very strongly that violence and terror will resolve nothing, no matter who you are or what your cause is. Violence breeds more violence, and we cannot attain our goals through violent acts. In fact, it's quite the opposite—violence only causes more aggravation and more problems for everyone.

As a Jordanian Arab, I am completely and utterly opposed to what happened on September 11th. I don't know whether it was al Qaeda or someone else behind it, but it was very inhumane, very ruthless, very violent, and uncalled for.

Unfortunately, there are people who use certain causes in the Arab world and in the Middle East to justify their personal agendas and ways of life. I personally do not agree with any form of religious fundamentalism—be it Muslim, Arab, or Western Christian. When I hear the way some of the leaders of the U.S. government talk I get scared as a citizen of the world. They scare me because they are very narrow-minded in their approach and very fundamentalist in their views, and this is creating more Osama bin Ladens all over the world. These Americans are planting the seeds of anger, which grow daily by the thousands and create supporters for violent fundamentalists like bin Laden. I would like to tell all religious fundamentalists and leaders everywhere that violence—no matter when or where it originates—begets more violence and more hatred, and widens the gap of understanding between peoples.

Dialogue is the only way to bring about peace—dealing with the root cause. I think terrorism takes place for several reasons. Purist ideologues who believe in a certain way of life feel that change comes through revolution, not evolution. They believe that they know best and want people to follow them, so they use terror to enforce their political agendas. But terrorism is fueled by real injustices repeatedly suffered by real people. This mobilizes followers. So if there is a case like the Palestinian one it can easily be used by every "Tom, Dick, and Harry" in the Arab and Islamic world to mobilize their anger. Killing innocent civilians in the name of any cause is not acceptable to any religion, which is something that all people need to be educated about.

And this should be the biggest role of the United States. When the U.S. says it's fighting terror, I say good. But you need to do crisis *resolution*—not crisis management. What the U.S. is doing now is periodically managing the crisis, but not eliminating the root cause.

We need to do more. We need to figure out why these organizations are forming and growing, why they're getting sympathy, and why they're getting support at the grassroots level. We need to get to the root and deal with the causes of the problem, not just the symptoms. Explaining terrorism in simple untruthful terms like, "They do this because they hate us and are jealous of us and our freedom," is completely misleading and will never lead to peace.

*   *   *

We have one paramount problem in the Arab world: the Palestinians. The Arab-Israeli-Palestinian struggle has been going on for over fifty years and there is no resolution in sight. The region has endured decades and decades of agony and suffering because of this problem. The Palestinians are the only people in the whole world today who are stateless, and this is unacceptable. By ignoring the injustice committed against the Palestinians, the world is giving bin Laden and others the justification to carry on and enhancing their ability to get more support from the Arab world.

We acknowledge that it's a two-way street—as Arabs we have a responsibility to come to terms with our own mistakes, whether as Arab governments or Arab people. I know in my heart that once we do that we can handle all our problems in a better manner. But the Palestinian problem has become too complicated, and there are grave responsibilities that rest on the shoulders of the . West, on the American administration and Europeans.

The U.S. especially needs to play the role of the honest broker correctly. We cannot go from the Clinton era where the administration was totally engaged at the highest levels and was so close to reaching some kind of solution, to a Bush administration that is totally disengaged. It went from one extreme to the other, from total engagement to zero engagement. This is not the way to deal with foreign policy. You cannot fluctuate in such a drastic manner when you have a vested interest in this conflict. To proclaim that you are partners with us in the Middle East you need to put your money where your mouth is, take a stand, and work with the legitimate leaders of the Arab world.

It's time for the United States to wake up and address the root causes of the unfortunate incident of September 11th. The U.S. needs to face the reality that these fundamentalists use the daily injustices perpetrated against the Palestinians to recruit young minds from the Arab world to commit violent acts.

Now the same scenario is happening in Iraq. When Arabs see Israeli tanks in occupied Gaza and American tanks in Faluja, Iraq these images are negatively imprinted on our minds, causing resentment that could create a serious backlash in our societies.

*   *   *

I don't want Americans reading this to misunderstand me. The U.S. is like a second home to me; I lived there for six years and know that many Americans do not know much about the outside world. I do not blame them because they live on a continent of their own, but things are different now. Living in a democracy means having an empowered people who are informed enough to make good decisions, but to do this people need the right information and free access to that information. This is why unbiased and truthful information is imperative for the sustainability and continuity of the U.S. democracy and any democracy. Americans need to know more about the Arab people from the Arab people themselves—not through anti-Arab stereotypes.

When I started my freshman college year in Ohio people around me were surprised to know that I was a Christian Arab. They assumed that I went to school on the back of a camel and they used to ask me the stereotypical questions that most Arabs are asked. I used to laugh and explain things to them. Some of my friends in college visited me in Jordan, and they were actually surprised to see that Jordan was a modern country combining what is fine in the East with what is fine in the West.

Some readers might find it strange that as a Jordanian Christian I am talking about the Palestinians with passion. My mother is from Jerusalem and my father is from a Jordanian East Bank city called Madaba. This intermarriage between Jordanians and Palestinians created a new generation that has a keen interest in both identities and an instinct to preserve those identities. All of us in the Arab world define ourselves as Arab citizens—Jordanian Arabs, Syrian Arabs, Egyptian Arabs, and so on—so the Palestinians are just a natural extension of our Arab identity. They are part of the Arab world and we live with them on a day-to-day basis, especially here in Jordan.

Jordan hosts the largest number of Palestinian refugees. They fled into Jordanian territory during the 1948, 1967, and 1973 wars. We grew up seeing their suffering, and it is frustrating that the suffering is increasing instead of decreasing. I know that it might be difficult for Americans to understand why all Arabs care this much about the Palestinians, but the issue of Palestine has become part of our day-to-day life.

I'm a Catholic Christian, so the Vatican and the Pope are my reference points. As human beings, we can disagree on translations of the Bible and denominations—we have translated things in different ways over the centuries. I respect such differences, but nowhere have I seen in the Arab world or in the East a counterpart to the fundamentalist Christians in the United

States. I have not heard of it whatsoever in this part of the world, not at all. The way U.S. evangelicals think creates more division at a time where we need to be coming together.

This is why the interfaith dialogue is imperative. It should trickle down from the most senior people to the lowest ranks within religious groups. We need to encourage this, and we need to make it easier for people to see commonalities. We are far more alike as human beings than we are different, but unfortunately we are focusing on our few differences rather than our many similarities.

I believe that Jerusalem should be an international city, an open city governed by international law under special U.N. charter whereby there is no sovereignty except for God. This is a city that carries a lot of religious, historical, and political weight and for this reason Jerusalem should be kept out of the conflict. As a Christian and an Arab I believe that Jerusalem belongs to all religions of the world and should be an open and free city for all religions where each individual is allowed to practice religion freely.

*   *   *

I don't believe that most Americans are anti-Arab; I believe that most Americans lack awareness about the Arab world and that Arabs have failed miserably in delivering our message properly to the American public. We have not invested our money to build an awareness campaign in the West, particularly in the United States, to make people there more aware of everything that is good about the Arab culture. After all, Arab culture is the cradle of civilization. We excelled in astronomy and established it as a science. We created algebra and the concept of zero. We excelled in medicine, architecture, navigation, and geography. Anywhere you look you will find Arab contributions to civilization, and yet none of this is appreciated or even known to average Americans. This is really our fault as Arabs.

The fact remains that we have failed drastically as Arab countries and as Arab people to convey the right message to

Americans and this is because we are a divided people. Arab countries are not united, which benefits those who want to see us regress as a people and as a civilization. We need to start to do things differently in the Arab world to meet the challenges we are facing now.

Another reason that knowledge about Arabs isn't reaching the American people is the American media. It seems as if this media is bent on reinforcing the typical stereotypes of Arabs. I work in the garment business and just got back from a business trip to the United States. I work with Calvin Klein, Kenneth Cole, Perry Ellis, and other major U.S. brand names and was terribly disappointed at the reaction I got from ordinary Americans.

I was walking in a Washington mall with a friend and speaking Arabic, and I noticed people staring at me. I had never felt this uncomfortable in the U.S. before. I was stunned by what I heard on American TV and radio. I noticed a lot of anti-Arabic attitude and sentiment in some political shows, and sometimes it was just blatant racism—racism against a whole people, not just those who acted on September 11th—and I felt that this is not the America that I know. It is different in so many ways. It is unfortunate that Americans now equate every Arab with terrorists, because the majority of the Arab world strongly condemned September 11th.

I feel it's unjust and unfair for the Arab identity to be treated this way; we deserve much better than this, from ourselves and from others.

I've been to the United States over fifty times, and this was the first time that I was kept for several hours at the airport being interrogated and asked silly questions that could never catch a terrorist, like: "Who do you know in the United States?" and "Why are you coming here?" etc. You think a terrorist is going to say, "Oh, I came here to commit a crime?" No way. I don't blame Americans for being more cautious about their security; it is their prerogative, but one cannot jump from one extreme to the other and think it is healthy for democracy. We need to learn to distinguish between terrorists and others, and the U.S. has the technology and the resources to do this.

It was a disturbing trip, and my heart goes out to all the Arab-Americans who are living there, including my family members who live in Michigan, Chicago, and Los Angeles. They tell me they feel very uncomfortable. It's so unfortunate for them to feel like this because this should not be happening in the great American democracy, the "melting pot" that brings together people from all over the world—people of all religions, colors, and ethnicities.

I worry that, God forbid, a bunch of lunatics will commit some other crime in the U.S. and that we'll see Arab-Americans being placed in concentration camps like the Japanese in WWII. I'm very concerned about this and believe that the American government needs to take steps to create more bridges between America and the Arab world.

*   *   *

What I like the most about the United States is that it is one of the few countries in the world that is a land of innovation. There is no limit! The sky is the limit for you to excel based on your merit, your abilities, and your performance.

I think that one reason why America excelled and reached this level of innovation is because it broke away from traditional taboos and inhibitions. It created an individualistic society where everyone has the chance to work hard. But, this took a toll on the family unit.

What I like most about being an Arab is the strong sense of belonging to a family unit. It gives one a sense of security that no matter how sick, poor, or old you become, there is a family out there that will take care of you. So everything has a price; to be innovative, U.S. society became less attached to the family unit, because being too attached to the family unit hindered innovation! Because of my family, I feel very safe living in this part of the world, but I know that many Americans feel that we are not safe here. I hear this all the time.

Three of my American colleagues from the garment business in New York just visited. After spending a few days in Amman, one of them laughed and said, "I feel safer here than in New York." So I think it's an over-exaggeration to say that the Arab world is not safe, because if you look at the number of crimes that happen in New York City versus the number that occur in the whole country of Jordan, you will find that Jordan ranks a thousand times better than New York City in safety.

Americans may think the Arab world is unsafe because of the war in Iraq, which complicates matters. I think it was an unfounded war, and even U.S. Secretary of State Colin Powell ultimately denied that there were any weapons of mass destruction in Iraq. The same man who made the case for war in front of the U.N. Security Council denied the very premise that the U.S. used to convince the world to go to war in Iraq! Look at Iraq now. It went from a police state to a lawless state where terror organizations roam freely. I hope that the new interim government will be able to bring order to Iraq.

I definitely do not think America should withdraw now; it will be disastrous if they do. There must be a viable political and administrative mechanism put in place before they leave or a civil war might break out in Iraq. I hope that destabilization was not the reason the United States went into Iraq. It's something that boggles my mind. We talk about security in the region, we talk about preservation of U.S. interests within the region, yet the U.S. took every step to jeopardize all that. Why?

If I saw President Bush in person I would ask him tough questions and tell him that the money he spent on the Iraq War and the destruction of that country would have created ten Palestinian states, enhanced Israel's security for a hundred years to come, and created a very prosperous Middle East. It would have eliminated a great root cause of terrorism.

I would tell President Bush that he is not serving America's interest with this war and is heading the wrong way. I would say,

"Just imagine what would have happened had you invested all these billions of dollars and manpower in building a prosperous Middle East? Where would we all be now?"

This is something that really bothers me. When I read about how much the U.S. has spent on this war—$150 billion so far I think—and I read U.N. and E.U. studies that say that the whole Palestinian refugee problem could be resolved for $20 billion, I wonder who plans U.S. foreign policy! This only shows that Mr. Bush dragged the U.S. into Iraq for its oil; at least this was one of the major reasons for the war.

I believe that America is seeking a new strategy for the twenty-first century. The U.S. is camping in Afghanistan and controlling the oil pipelines that are very important for many countries in that region, especially China. Now they control Iraq, which has more oil reserves than Saudi Arabia. After all, oil is the lifeblood of the world economy, and whoever controls it controls the world economy and will become politically and militarily supreme.

I believe that there are many goals that America has achieved through its invasion of Iraq. It was not about Saddam Hussein, although none of us in the Arab world liked him. Historians will write about all this, and Americans will read those books. That's what I mean when I said earlier that Americans must have access to information. Had they known all this before the war perhaps they would have reacted differently.

If you believe in democracy and the right of self-determination and freedom then you should do the same for the Palestinian people. I ask every single American to think about this very hard and come up with an answer.

I would really like to ask the American people this: How can you support your president in such a baseless war? Every day brings evidence that proves the war was based on lies, and this evidence

comes from Americans, historians, strategists, and intelligence experts. How can you support such a war, but not find it in your heart to give that same level of support to resolving the Palestinian problem?

Enas on location

Enas, 49
Film Director
Cairo, Egypt
Muslim

Americans and Arabs need to start talking *to* each other—
rather than *at* each other. If Americans merely insist on their
opinion and we on ours, it will be difficult to achieve a mutual
understanding.

Introduction

Meeting Enas was pure coincidence. I went to a Cairo gym
that overlooked the Nile in an effort to work off some calories
from the unbelievable amount of rich, delicious food I had been
consuming every day since my plane landed in the Arab world.
More accurately, I was *on* a gym—a gym boat. It was an old barge
that had been remodeled and, although anchored, was now literally
floating in the Nile River delta.

As I finished my workout, I noticed a tall, attractive woman
walking on the treadmill. She had very light brown hair and was
even taller than me. She seemed strangely familiar—although I
could not remember where I might have seen her before. Was she
someone I had known during my college days at the American
University in Cairo? Or someone I had seen on TV or read about
in magazines? I asked one of the attendants about her and was told
that she was Enas, the first Arab woman to gain prominence as a
cinematic director.

The journalist in me immediately thought of how great it
would be to interview her. Then I started to wonder if she was

really such a good candidate for my book. I had originally decided not to seek out individuals who were well known, because I wanted to represent the views of typical Arabs similar to those Americans who had posed the questions I used in the interviews. But I had not sought this woman out; coming across her was purely coincidental. Besides, what she might say was likely to surprise my American audience. I feared she would probably just give me a nasty look and turn down my request for an interview, but I decided it was at least worth a try.

Much to my surprise, when I approached her she simply smiled and said, "Of course you can interview me!"

Although I had been working out for nearly an hour, at that moment my heart really began to race. I could not believe it. Instead of my accidental subject, it was *me* who had been caught off guard.

Enas gave me her phone number and I called her later that day. She asked me to meet her on the following Monday at 9:00 p.m. in her office. She worked in a building that was not too far from where I was staying.

I arrived that Monday at exactly 9:00. Before I was shown into the office, her male assistant asked me what I wanted to drink. I should note that he did not ask *if* I wanted something to drink— declining a drink when you visit someone is considered impolite and unacceptable behavior in the Arab world. As I waited for him to bring me a cup of hot tea, I glanced into Enas's office where she paced back and forth as she talked on the phone. She saw me and smiled, gesturing politely. To my astonishment, I realized she was not wearing any make-up. Furthermore, she was dressed very casually in pants and a t-shirt. This alone spoke volumes about my interview subject. To be a successful woman in the Arab world without conforming to cultural constraints is relatively uncommon.

Enas was the eighth person I interviewed. Her interview made me feel sure that the book would become a reality and perhaps be successful not only in America, but also in the Arab world. I had already begun to feel that the book would stir up more controversy in Arab countries than in the United States. Enas made me certain of this. Her honesty was brutal. Although she does not know it, I want to be a film director like her some day—although my focus will be documentaries.

The main benefit of my interview with Enas is that it shows Americans a side of Arab women they rarely see—a successful Arab woman who can be very critical of certain aspects of her culture, yet remain very proud of the overall culture and of Islam. She is someone who made it against great odds in her own territory, within her own culture, and without being a sell-out. You can disagree with her, but you cannot help but respect her.

Meet Enas

I grew up in a middle-class family. As they say here in Egypt, "Parents who were simple and religious raised me." There were eight children in my family. My father taught Arabic at a local school, but my mother did not work. She had completed elementary school and could read and write. She read quite a bit about her political interests—but she did not have a higher education.

Of eight children, I was the only girl. It was quite a struggle, and we were all expected to pull our own weight. There was no pampering in our household. Our parents did not coddle any of us. Despite his limited resources, my father had one primary goal: to teach us the importance of education—and he succeeded. He and my mother worked really hard to ensure that the eight of us graduated from universities and had good jobs. My brothers work in medicine, engineering, and science. I am the only one who chose a profession in the arts.

In the beginning, when I started working in cinema, I faced rejection from my conservative family. They were afraid the field of cinema was overly liberal and had too many problems. This type of thinking didn't originate with my parents; it was the general impression of people in Egypt.

It took me a while before I managed to overcome these reservations. Eventually, I enrolled in the production department at the Cinema Institute, but soon changed my major to directing. I never considered acting, since I knew this would make my family quite angry; their primary fear was that I would become an actress.

I graduated in the mid-1970s and co-directed films with various directors who were important in Egypt at that time. Ten years later, I decided the time had come to work for myself—to introduce myself as a director. So I decided to direct my own movie, which I called *Sorry Law*.

I did not fully realize my interests at the time, but my choice for the film's story was telling. It focused on a law in Egypt that I considered to be particularly unfair. This law had to do with crimes related to adultery. If a man caught his wife in bed with another man and he killed her, the crime would be, according to this law, a minor offense. But if the same situation happened with a woman and she killed her husband, it would be considered a felony. This was a huge discrepancy.

I always asked why the criminal law differentiated between men and women in terms of killing and betrayal, while the Islamic law that Egypt follows did not. The unfair distinction has nothing to do with Islamic law. It has everything to do with the fact that the Egyptian and broader Muslim society is male-dominated and committed to the notion that men are somehow better than women. I constantly questioned why we didn't apply God's doctrine—one that is truly fair—to both men and women.

I believe that men have circumvented God's laws and changed the interpretation of Islam as it pertains to crimes committed by women. True Islam is totally different from that which is practiced in the present. I felt that if the Prophet were alive today, he would change much of the writings from earlier centuries because, being a rational person, he would see how life has evolved and adjust his teachings accordingly.

I started my work from this premise and the finished film was popular with the people. Initially, there was some criticism from males. They said, "What do you want to do—encourage adultery in our society?" They did not see that I merely wished to promote equality between men and women. There were a lot of arguments and criticisms concerning the film. Eventually, all the criticism worked in the film's favor. The controversy provoked people to want to see it. The debate also classified me as a cause-oriented director. My second film focused on the problems associated with drug use. No controversy arose from that story.

Having directed fourteen films, I've found my most important ones are those addressing the causes of women and the societal inequality women face. I often focus entirely on female characters and make their struggles the main theme. I also tend to show all aspects of women's struggles, trying to be as thorough and realistic as possible. I've been attacked a lot for doing this, and very often the attacks have come from women. Unfortunately, many women's societies and organizations have not wanted to see women portrayed in unfavorable situations in movies.

Even today, women's groups still want to see women portrayed in a "proper" way or to see an image of how women ought to be, and not how women really are. They do not want to face the uncomfortable side of reality. Yet drama in general shows both the good and bad face of reality. There are positive and negative issues and situations facing women and we must show all sides so that people can see the differences for themselves.

I directed a film called *One Woman Is Not Enough*. In the film, I display the upbringing of an Eastern man. He loves three women and his society does not seem to mind. Eventually, the man faces a choice; he must decide which woman to marry. He agonizes over the decision and eventually chooses the one that is furthest from his thoughts and interests. In other words, he picks the wrong woman to be his wife. Why? Because the most important factor in his decision-making process was that he had never had a sexual relationship with the woman he chose to marry. To him, that was most essential.

This concept angered some women's groups. I wasn't sure what made them so angry. It was not as though I had shown him deciding to marry three women or something. The only point the movie illustrated was that a man could have a relationship with three women and finally pick one of them to be his wife based solely on the fact that he had not had a physical relationship with her. I wanted to show how the upbringing of the Eastern man is different from the upbringing of the Eastern woman. This upbringing is part of our society and we have to examine it; we must not ignore it.

I do not aim to be prejudiced in favor of women. All I do in my movies is focus on an issue that exists in society, but is seldom discussed. Lately in Egypt many people have become more conservative and a growing number of Islamic religious organizations oppose efforts such as mine. In my case, they don't want to see a woman who talks openly about sex and mores. They believe I have broken away from tradition and that, as a woman, I have crossed the line. In a way, maybe this is true. I am a woman who talks about taboo subjects, and I have sex scenes in my movies—just like male Arab directors.

I have the courage to bluntly call for women's rights—both material and moral. But I do not worry much about the material rights. It would be useless to call for material rights for women before we free them morally. What use is it if I earn the same salary as a man, but the society looks at me as something totally different, something without feelings or sensations—a woman who was created merely as a body for her husband to enjoy?

I've faced severe attacks from Egyptian society. Even some Arab news media have participated in these attacks, especially one media outlet that is known to be prejudiced and connected to several religious groups. Modern media everywhere seem to be increasingly based more on slander and excitement than on truth. The attacks have reached a level where people admonish me without even having seen my films. I tend not to worry too much about these assaults on my reputation. I believe in what I do and know that I am capable of reaching the people and that there are a lot of people who respect me. They might not be the majority, but they see things the way I see them. So far, the behavior of many such people has proven that I am not wrong.

Soon after I began working in the film industry, it was no longer necessary for my family to help me because I had become financially independent. This was extremely uncommon in Egypt in the 1970s. Unmarried daughters—even those that worked—remained financially dependent on their families. This dependence gave parents the ability to interfere with their daughters' lives. To a lesser extent, this was even true for unmarried sons.

Therefore, I faced a considerable problem with my family, not just because I was financially independent, but also because I lived alone in a separate house, which they considered to be completely unacceptable. This created quite a conflict between my parents and me.

I was in love with my husband for nine years before we finally got married. This was not an easy thing to do in Egypt. Egyptian women marry the man of their choice; however, family approval of their choice is very important. The man is expected to walk into her house and propose to her family, rather than her. We did not do any of that.

This was the most important period of my life in terms of work and character development. I've always said that a successful woman must succeed both in her work and in her personal life. Many times women who fail in their personal lives become very sad and feel that a major part of their lives are lost. I am not in favor of the woman who succeeds in her work at the expense of her personal life, nor with the one who succeeds in her personal life at the expense of her work. Neither of these is real success, in my view.

The real success of a woman is measured by a difficult equation, one which is built on a balance between work and personal life. If a woman manages to solve this equation, only then can I say: that is a successful woman. This is what I tried to do in my life. That is why I got married after being in love and living with my husband for nine years.

We had some other problems, too. He was a Christian and I was a Muslim. This is a tough issue in our society, because Muslim women are supposed to marry Muslim men. For us this is the law. So he had to convert to Islam in order for the marriage to happen. This was another one of the many problems I've had with

my family. How could I think of getting married to a Christian?
They are convinced that he became a Muslim only for the purpose
of marriage and not because he truly believed in Islam.

Though this has been a problem, it has been completely
worth it. My husband's thinking is totally different from that of
the typical Eastern man. He has given me the freedom to work and
the freedom to go out. He does not ask me to be a housewife, nor
demand that I do all of the cooking and cleaning. All of this has
helped me considerably. The fact that my husband is not a
traditional Egyptian or Arab man has helped my career
considerably.

*   *   *

I cannot say exactly why I see things so differently from
many other Arab women; I'm not sure what the specific reasons
are. One reason could be the home I grew up in. There was some
prejudice against me and in favor of the boys. This prejudice was
created by my mother. Everything relating to boys was different.
Dealing with the newly born, celebrations, everything.

My mother—like most women in this society—considered
her sons to be an asset to the family, while I was only a girl. She
never actually said that boys were better, but it was clear she felt
they came first and girls second. But maybe this only exists in my
mind. It is possible that I just wanted to prove that boys are not
superior. Maybe I just wanted to be a leader and do whatever I felt
like, regardless of whether I was boy or a girl.

Perhaps working in the film industry has made me
different. Being a movie director is a difficult profession, but I
love it. This job has had a significant effect on my character.
When I was younger I did not feel very optimistic or confident. I
did not even realize it then, but I do now. I've come to realize that
everything in life has a goal. Why should I stop when I face
hurdles? Why should I stop whatever I am doing every time I
encounter something that bothers me?

I think being a director has made me stronger emotionally. I do not tend to feel extremely happy or extremely sad. I am always somewhere in the middle. Life trains you to be in control of your emotions. I have ended up doing what I want and not what others want or expect of me. I've always had an inner feeling—an insight, if you will—that what I choose to do is correct. I make mistakes just like everyone else, but their impact on my overall confidence has always been limited.

I have inherited some things from my father. He was very fair, always spoke the truth and did what he considered right— even when it related to his sons. I have the same personality as his.

*   *   *

I was born in an important time in the history of modern Egypt. I spent my youth in the 1970s. It was a rich period in Egypt. Egyptians were open to the West. We had no complications and there were no Muslim movements or extremism. Socialism, capitalism, dreams for change, and Gamal Abdel Nasser [Nationalist leader of Egypt and the Arab world] were all a part of my youth and helped build my personality without me even noticing.

There was a vibrant atmosphere amongst the youth at the Cinema Institute. We constantly saw the socialists, capitalists, and others arguing and debating their ideas and ideals. I attended many public lectures and often used to go to the "Reesh" coffee shop (a famous café in Egypt where intellectuals of all political colors would meet). I never took sides or even participated in the debates, but I was a part of this important era of political discussion and saw it all happen right before my eyes.

All of that contributed to the building of my character. The intellectual atmosphere of the Cinema Institute, being a director, my family, and the need to be strong and successful have all made me who I am. Even being a co-director had an impact on my personality, because I was a woman working with great Egyptian directors and felt I needed to work harder to prove myself and find my footing.

I was not necessarily treated differently because I was a woman. Some people talk of managers who put certain pressure on women who work with them, but I never faced this in my work. I have never obtained a job or a business opportunity based on being female in a man's world. I do my work correctly and this is why I am respected. I am not well-known because I am a woman, but because of the quality of my work. People do not just see me as a beautiful woman and judge me accordingly. My beauty will eventually disappear and what I will be left with is my work and what I've achieved in my lifetime.

I really have not experienced any sexual harassment. I live in an Eastern society and work in a totally different job from most women here—one that was not conquered by women when I started working in it. I have never had a special relationship with anyone I worked with. I have always felt that it is important to keep one's personal life away from work so as not to jeopardize either one.

*   *   *

I come from a religious home, but I judge all religions with my mind. I do not take anything for granted and do not just accept things as they are. I like Islam not only because it is a religion, but also because it is a way of life. It is a religion that has laws but allows plenty of space for people to make mistakes. Islam is flexible and it's not the end of the world if someone violates a rule or teaching of Islam. There is always a space for forgiveness and repentance. People do not follow Islam to the letter. It is an easygoing religion. Even the interpretations are flexible. It does not have one specific interpretation like other religions. I like that.

There are many things that I like about Arab culture. I love the warm close relations between people. I like the unique warmth of Eastern peoples, which remains intact no matter what happens. There are beautiful relations between relatives, friends, and neighbors. Whatever happens to you as an individual, you never feel alone. Especially here in Egypt, you will never feel that you are lonely. You also feel that when you have a problem, there will be someone there to comfort you.

I've even found comfort during periods of extreme criticism from the press. Actually, the press has played a role that I consider to have been in my favor. When they attacked me, they helped create "Enas—The Movie Director." They made the public aware of my existence. I even sometimes played the cat and mouse game with the media and waited to see who would eat whom.

*   *   *

As I told you before, my job has made me a perpetual optimist. I believe in faith and I believe that we are predestined. If things are going to happen, they will. If not, they won't. I was once on the hit list of an Islamic organization, which called for my assassination along with the President of Egypt and the Sheikh of al Azhar (the most prestigious Islamic institution in the Arab and Muslim world).

They put my name on the list because they claimed that I crossed too many lines and helped spread moral corruption throughout Islamic society. The government offered me round-the-clock protection, but I refused. "What good are guards?" I asked, "President Sadat of Egypt was killed while surrounded by a huge number of guards. All the protection in the world would not have saved him if he were pre-destined to die that day."

I did not feel that I had done something that required me to be guarded. It is true that the arts are effective, but their power is limited because the viewer chooses to reject or accept what is seen. Viewers can believe what they see or deny it and go on with their lives. I do not try to impose my ideas or turn them into laws. Therefore, I have never had an inner feeling that I need protection. God is the protector. I have great faith in God and believe if someone wants to kill me, I will be killed—even if a hundred thousand guards surround me.

*   *   *

Egyptian and Arab society have a warmth that I love, despite all the struggles and the unfavorable economic situation. In spite of recent events, Egyptians have something beautiful that has existed since the beginning of history. Ultimately, it is the people who always become united as one hand, regardless of the government. When the French occupied Egypt, we did not speak French. The same was true when the English and Turks occupied the country; we never changed our language. We've always spoken Arabic. Egyptians can even laugh and joke about their miserable conditions under all those occupations.

Many Egyptians do not care much about the outside world. But this is a double-edged weapon, both good and bad. If the people knew the reality, they would explode. So they prefer not to know. It is for this reason that Egyptian people laugh and joke and are always optimistic, even when hungry and poor. You feel that life is going on and that poverty is a normal part of life, like height or eye color.

I never wish I had been born somewhere else. I love to travel and see new places, but I could not live outside of Egypt. I am very proud of my country. I do not say this because I am talking to the media now. It is because my country has some of the greatest things in the world. It is true that we go through bad economic circumstances, but it is very difficult for one to imagine living away from his or her country. I travel to America, go sightseeing, and see all the development they have that may be transferred to us. They have democracy for themselves, but do not practice democracy with us.

As a woman, I have succeeded in my country because of personality, talent, and work ethic. I put things that bother me behind me and don't let them slow me down. You won't find any population that is totally happy with its country. Even Americans are not happy—Europeans either. There are problems in every country. I always say that a woman is a huge mass of will. If she wants to do something, she will do it. Nothing can challenge her or stop her—except herself. A woman who wants to stand up for her rights and be something must accomplish that in her own country and not somewhere else.

I do not feel like something is special when I go to the U.S. and do whatever I want. America gives everyone the right to do whatever he or she wants to do. But when I do that in my own country, I feel stronger than when I do it in America. Therefore, I consider a person's will to be very important. Things that are going on around you will pull you down a little. But you will be able to run the race and win it if you have the ability. I really wish that we had more freedom and economic prosperity here. I wish for many things. I wish that we would wake up from the political sleep we are in.

*   *   *

In my films, I try to provoke people and wake them up. But even life itself does not provoke some people. This does not mean that I should stop trying.

Once during dinner with a female friend from the cinema society, she asked me, "What should we do about our problems?"

I replied, "What problems?"

Here we were, eating fancy food at a special dinner, and this woman actually says to me, "The problems of Arab women."

This really annoyed me. I said, "I do not like this talk. Things do not change by words. Arab women should not cry over their problems and say they live tragic lives. They should work harder at changing whatever is annoying them. Each woman should try to change things in her own field. We should not just meet, start women's associations, complain, and organize demonstrations holding signs that say "NO." Show me in practice what you are doing to make change happen."

I refuse to join women's groups or believe that I must explain myself as a woman. I do not believe in sitting around and inventing mottos. Unfortunately, women in this country seem to be more interested in talk than in action. You know what tragedy is? It is to be a successful woman working in medicine, the movie industry, journalism, education, or business and see the wheel of women's success rolling along, yet sit and complain and cry over the women's tragedy. What tragedy are we really talking about when we can do so many marvelous and successful things?

Being a director in Egypt did not exist for women before me. When I became a director, this became a profession that women began to look up to. Young girls started saying: "I want to be a director like Enas."

I am looked up to because I did what I wanted and made a dream come true. I did it myself and did not wait for any women's group to make it happen for me. At the same time, I took care of my appearance and my personal life. In me, young women see an Arab woman who can be a serious director and at the same time, become a model in society and live her life freely. I am a role model. I am not interested in organizing rallies or joining associations.

When I get invited to meetings with women, I often decline. With all due respect, I cannot stand to listen to their moaning and crying over how desperate the situation is. There are many examples outside of Egypt of women who made change happen. But here we are doing nothing. We just sit and say that we live in a tragedy. What about the Arab women in countries that still lack freedom? Women in Egypt, Syria, Lebanon, and Jordan gained freedom a long time ago. Women in these countries should be governing by now.

I do not see that crying over our problems is an important aspect of women's issues. Women should conquer every field of work and do their best to succeed. Every woman should try on her own to succeed in whatever she is doing. Only then will women feel they truly exist. Women's associations merely create problems. We are not against men. We want to walk side-by-side along the same road and not to be less than or better than them. We want to walk together. No one should have a higher rank than another.

Proving myself through my work gives me an identity of my own and, therefore, enables me to truly exist. This is the preeminent need for Arab and Egyptian women, to find their own identity by themselves.

         *   *   *

Western movies and television tend to only show the traditional appearance of Arabs. They either show Arab women in traditional dress or wearing a dancing costume. They show men in long garments—as if all Arab men wear Gulf-style attire. They don't. Foreign movies make Arabs look very different and strange to Westerners.

If a Western movie showed an Arab woman who was similar to Western women and wore the same clothes they wear, there wouldn't be anything compellingly "foreign." Therefore, Arab women are always shown with a totally different appearance than we actually have. Western films do not show real Arab women or their achievements.

I like America and have been there many times. People think Americans are bad, but they are actually quite nice. For example, many small things move me when I am walking down the street in America. You find nicely dressed people who talk to one another and say a lot of complimentary things to perfect strangers. In fact, I have never been to a country where people talk to you and give you a compliment if you are beautiful. If you are in an elevator people smile. I see Americans as kind people. They act homogenously, even though they come from different origins. I love the progress that exists in America and the people who work hard and honestly. All of that exists in America and we cannot deny it.

America is a great country, although we feel they are taking a negative position against Arabs at present. What is going on

now, however, is related to the current political period, and we
cannot judge the whole American nation solely on recent events.
We cannot say America is a bad country because they are against
us. A person should be aware of what is good there and appreciate
it. As a country, America is beautiful. Many beautiful things exist
there and there is a tremendous amount of variety. Each state has
its own richness and many beautiful things. But as a government,
and at this particular period, we are angry at America.

We feel that the American government is against us. We
also feel they are being unjust with Arabs in a strange way. We
are puzzled by the behavior of the American government. They
are the ones who once supported the very people they now identify
as their enemies. America helped create Saddam Hussein and
supported Islamic resistance movements in Afghanistan. If it
weren't for the backing of the United States, neither of them would
ever have gained power. Therefore, it is not us who should be
blamed for what went wrong; it is the fault of an American
government that creates dictators, uses them, and then throws them
away.

This is what I do not like about America. It used these
people for certain purposes, took advantage of them, and then
turned against them and went to war to get rid of them. What I do
not like about America is that it has been unjust in issues that
pertain to Arabs. Yes, each country looks after its own interests,
but protecting interests does not necessitate false accusations. This
is what is now being done with Arabs.

I do not think this policy is a result of September 11th. It
has been going on for some time now. September 11th was just an
event that made it clear. This tragedy occurred as a result of
America's support of religious extremism (during the Soviet
invasion of Afghanistan). Religion is becoming more of an issue
in American politics, and I reject that.

Nowadays, you hear the word "Muslim" everywhere. You
hear terms like "Islamic nations"—not Arab nations. You hear
new expressions that did not exist before which are related to
religion. Suddenly everyone is either a Jew or a Muslim. Our

fight with Israel is not because they are Jews. Arabs are cousins of the Jews. Ignorant people do not know the difference. Jews are more related to Muslims than to Christians[1,2].

So the matter has become more religious rather than political. But America supported religious movements and strengthened Islamic groups when they needed them in their wars against the Soviets. We entered a religious war, which is the nastiest thing, and which takes us back to the Dark Ages. Wars are a political thing, but when they become religious, this will lead to the destruction of the world, which is in no one's interest.

I strongly believe in separating religion from politics. Religion is the relationship between man and God, which is a personal relationship. I was raised in a society that has Muslims and Christians. We have millions of Egyptian Copts (Christians) in our society. My friends and I never ask each other about religion. I might see a friend for a year and not know if she is a Muslim or a Christian. Therefore, I believe that religion is separate from politics. Some people might consider this as a sort of parting with Islamic tradition. But this is what I believe. My relationship is with God directly. Only God will judge me when I do not fast or pray. It does not mean that I am a non-believer. I am free to believe as I want. God will judge me later. Yet sometimes people want to judge now.

Terrorism is about the person and not his or her religion. It is also about poverty and injustice. Both can lead to anything in life. If I am hungry and I need to feed my hungry kids, I might kill my own brother. And if I feel someone is supporting a tyrant who

---

[1] From a Muslim perspective, Arabs are descendents of the Prophet Ishmael (PBUH) and Jews are descendents of the Prophet Isaac (PBUH). Ishmael and Isaac were brothers, the sons of Prophet Ibraheem (PBUH). Accordingly, Arabs and Jews are blood cousins.

[2] In 1781 the German scholar A. L. Schlozer coined the term "Semitic" to identify a family of related languages including Arabic, Hebrew, and Aramaic. He derived the word from "Sam" (Shem in Hebrew), one of the three sons of the Prophet Noah (PBUH).

is abusive toward me, then I might want to seek revenge against this supporter.

Violence comes as a result of injustice. What is going on in Iraq is injustice. Feeling that you are oppressed leads to terrorism. In Egypt, the source of violence is poverty. If the Islamic groups were well off and had more freedom they would not be fighting the government. It is their feeling of oppression that drives and motivates them. They see the few who are very rich as having taken everything, leaving the rest with nothing to eat. This can lead them to violence. In Egypt, I think it's the economic situation that leads some people to violence.

The case is the same for the Palestinians. They are oppressed in their own country. They have no rights in their own home and this leads them to violence. They do not find anyone on their side. This makes them even more violent. If someone ended the oppression of the Palestinians and gave them their rights, 90% of the violence would disappear and only natural human violence, such as criminal activity, would remain.

I cannot offer a clear-cut solution to the Palestine/Israel problem. This is a very difficult issue and the struggle of a whole generation. There is also oppression from the big countries of the West. They take the side of the Israelis. If the West dealt justly with the Palestinians, there would be much less violence. But when people feel they are always treated unjustly and that their opposition is always supported and made stronger, leading to further abuse, how can you possibly expect less violence? There is no balance. If the Palestinians felt a sense of balance, they would behave differently.

*   *   *

I do not know if there is hope for the region in relation to the war in Iraq, though I am optimistic. It is a huge epidemic. It will take time to cure everyone. Maybe if America withdraws from Iraq and leaves the people to live on their own the problem could begin to be solved. The U.S. does not really need to be physically inside Iraq; they have the power to control it from the outside. Why wouldn't they leave the people to live in peace? There might still be problems and pressure put on the Iraqis from the outside, but at least the problem would become an internal issue.

We all know the Iraq war is being fought over wealth and oil. It is the struggle for an area that is rich in natural resources. If our area was not rich, it would be a much quieter, more normal area with little violence, terrorism, or war. The solution may be for us to become poor and for the Americans and the West to take the wealth and leave us alone.

Many Americans are not happy with their government— and President Bush in particular—or with what is happening to Arabs and Muslims. Of course, these Americans have a role to play in their own country, especially since they have democracy. America is currently forming an empire. This cannot be achieved without terror, violence, and war.

The American people can change that; they can stop this dangerous empire-building. This might be achieved in the coming elections. They may not re-elect Bush, but even if they do not it is questionable whether the opposing candidate will be any different. But perhaps a new president might be different. He might not want to promote religious warfare, which is what Bush is doing now.

The religious struggles and wars that are taking place are terrible. It is most difficult to have to defend your religion from slanderous attacks and to be labeled a terrorist for doing so. Things other than religion can be evaluated through logic, but when it comes to religion, much is judged on the basis of passion and emotion rather than logic.

Americans do not need to agree with Arabs 100%, support them, or even like them—it is fine with us if they don't. But when America slanders Islam, this provokes us. Even non-religious Arabs will turn into extremists in reaction to such slander.

America does not seem to have a long-term vision of the future. All of the American presidents of recent years have supported Israel. They only try to support the Arabs just before their presidency is over. It is a dirty game of politics and religion should not be part of it.

Americans can play a role in changing this attitude, with their numbers, will, democracy, and feeling that they are part of the governing body. We Arabs, unfortunately, are people who lack such a feeling to the extent that we do not take part in elections. Even if we go to the elections we know that we will not be part of the ruling elite. We are now used to the cheating that comes with elections; our government is forced down our throats and imposed on us. Therefore, many of us simply withdraw from political participation. But Americans are capable of making a difference. They can force change through elections and through internal pressure on their government to change its unjust policies.

*   *   *

Americans and Arabs need to start talking *to* each other—rather than *at* each other. If Americans merely insist on their opinion and we on ours, it will be difficult to achieve mutual understanding. It will take time, but we Arabs must get used to participating in politics. We suffer from political depression and oppression. We are a people who look forward to genuine political participation at the global level. We understand what is going on, but not the whole story of nation-building, democracy, and politics.

We need to change the way we conduct things. When we sit together and discuss things in the Arab League we achieve no results. There are always fights and cursing and the meetings end without anything getting done. That is because we are somewhat inept when it comes to practicing politics freely. We need time to get used to free debates and open discussion. We have a lot to learn. We should learn how to debate at universities—maybe even when we learn the alphabet. We may need a little longer to become free because we were silent for so many years. We have this false impression that we cannot do anything, so we think the initiative should come from America.

We need an "older brother," from a humanitarian point of view, who will take care of his younger brother and teach him what to do without taking advantage of him. America talks about changing the world and making it better for all nations so we can all enjoy stability. But America should teach people how to do that without provoking them, slandering their culture and religion, and treating them unjustly. We lack a lot of things that we need to learn. We should admit this fact, because if we do not we will never achieve anything.

I do not take part in the elections and I do not have an election card, because I know that even if I gave my opinion, it would not be heard. I should not be like this. I should get an election card. I should go out and vote for whomever I want and give my opinion freely. But I need my vote to be counted and I need the results to be honest. I do not want to be fooled. I am an educated person and a proud woman. I should have a vote that is taken into consideration.

A long time ago, my mother had an election card and she used to take part in the elections, believing her vote would really make a difference. When she realized the impossibility of the actual results, which were consistently 99.9% in favor of the incumbent, she gave up on voting, even though there was a fine for not doing so. How could people see such results and still consider the elections fair?

If Americans feel they can bring hope to the rest of the world and that they have the ability to change the world, then they need to do so. But they need to do it the right way and not through war. I do not think America is a bloody nation or a criminal one. If someone dies in the United States, it is seen as a real disaster, whereas thousands could die here and we would not care because we consider this normal.

There is some genuine dialogue between both sides. When we go to America we talk. I went to America after September 11th. People here told me not to go because I would be insulted and detained, but this did not happen to me. It might have been true for others, but I did not experience it. Maybe it was because I do not look like a terrorist or wear the *hijab* (head covering worm by Muslim women).

When an American director made a film about Arab women, I was discussed, although I did not have any personal contact with them. They portrayed me as a character with a personal opinion of her country. I do not have any negative relations with America or any other country. I could go anywhere and learn new things because the world is small. The world is becoming one country. It's possible that everything being done now will pave the way for the world to become one strong nation in the future.

Americans have too little information about Arabs. They think all Arab women are beaten and have no rights. This comes as a result of arrogance. They should study more about others. Now that the world is so open and accessible, one should, at the very least, watch TV to learn more about other nations.

The one question I have for the ordinary American is, "Don't you feel that America is becoming a tyrant and not applying justice toward other nations?"

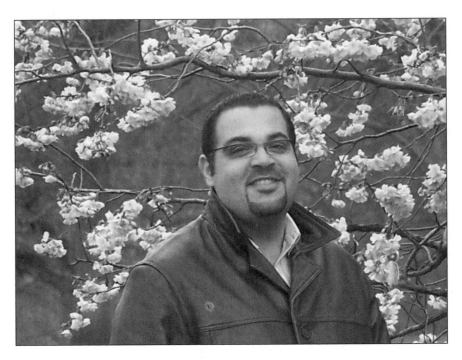

Osama enjoying the spring blossoms

Osama, 32
Financial Manager
Cairo, Egypt
Christian

If a young man cannot get a job, doesn't have security, and has no future to plan for, then he will lean toward fanaticism to change his situation....Some people think, 'If I can't live with dignity, then I might as well die for something.' They try to be a martyr for God. This might explain why some people support bin Laden.

Introduction

Osama was my first candidate for interviews in Cairo, Egypt. As I had done in Amman and Kuwait, I mentioned to people the purpose of the book, and that in Cairo I was looking for young Egyptians, both Muslim and Christian. A friend suggested several people, one of whom was Osama, who called me after he finished work one evening to get directions to my sister's house. His voice was extremely deep, and I started to get upset at the friend who had recommended Osama for my book. I wanted to be sure the thoughts of younger Arabs were represented in these interviews, and his voice made him sound much older.

However, the minute I opened the door I laughed and my anger melted. Osama was indeed young—as well as handsome, very tall, and with a goatee. I immediately assumed that he was Muslim, since his name carried a Muslim connotation for me. But soon after we started the interview, Osama told me, "I am a Christian."

I found it ironic that I, one who always asks people to be non-judgmental, assumed that Osama would be Muslim simply because of his name. How hard one must practice what one preaches!

The most interesting aspect about Osama was his keen interest in my project. He seemed very excited about it and felt that a conversation with Americans was necessary, despite the fact that he had never set foot in America, and seemed to know little about the country.

Meet Osama

My name is Osama, and I am thirty-two years old. I graduated from the school of architecture at Cairo University in 1994 and worked for six years in my field. But then I made many career changes that seem to be totally disconnected. I went into marketing and trading within the construction industry, and have been very lucky because I joined a multinational organization about a year and a half ago. I'm an assistant manager for Citibank assets in Egypt.

My father used to be the deputy chief editor for a newspaper. My mother had a brief career in fashion, but stopped working to care for my brother and me. She went back to work after I, the oldest, entered college, and now works in sales and marketing for one of the most famous Egyptian fashion designers. I have a brother who is a banker and a graduate of the American University of Cairo. He has been living in Canada for almost two and a half years, and works at the Nova Scotia Bank.

My hobbies are many and varied. For example, I love to walk, swim, and read. I'm very interested in the recent history of the Middle East and read a lot about this topic—mainly Arabic writers such as Hassanen Haikal. I am very interested in Islamic culture and history, and the Islamic religion. I take care to differentiate between the three because there are many aspects of these that get mixed, but should not. I also love to listen to music and would say my musical tastes are very eclectic. I can listen to almost any kind of music and enjoy it, but English music is my favorite.

I consider myself very lucky because I have traveled to many countries. I have been to Israel on business, Australia to visit relatives, Canada, France, Switzerland, and Jordan because my father worked there when I was twelve years old. I've even been to Senegal on a business trip. But no matter where I've traveled, I enjoyed the experiences.

Everywhere I go people ask me where I am from. I guess I have a strange accent that is not British, not American, and not really Arabic. It confuses people—especially in Italy, where everyone asked me where I came from! I told them "I'm an Egyptian." From this they often assumed I was Muslim. However, when I am abroad I am usually not asked what religion I am, and I am not really interested in raising the issue.

Even before September 11th I would say "I am from Egypt," because I was raised in Egypt. But it is a bit complicated to decide what I am. I think I am an Arab Egyptian. I didn't have a choice in this; I was born into the Arabic culture.

Despite my many travels, I have never been to the United States. I went to Canada and they did not give me any trouble entering or leaving in spite of my now infamous first name, "Osama." But I would love to visit the United States, especially to see New York. The U.S. is a new country and does not have many historical places to see, so I would visit the American Congress. Nobody visits the Congress in Egypt because we have a rich culture and many historical places to see. I would also love to visit the Vietnam Memorial because it's about war and history. It's about a lot of men who died for no reason—for a bad reason.

*   *   *

You say that Americans have posed the question: "Have you ever heard about Jesus Christ?" Of course, I have heard a lot about Jesus Christ since I was a child. I believe he is the son of

God and that he is God. I believe he was a man of peace, a man of love, and that he liberated us. I was raised to believe in God, but I don't practice religion. I do keep a very personal contact with God. I am a minority in this view, but I don't feel that it is a bad thing.

The people I know and work with never raise the issue of religion. If my best friends or the people that I socialize with are Christians, it is totally by coincidence. I do not go out of my way to befriend Christians. In fact, my best friends are Muslim, and they are the ones who introduced me to my Christian friends.

I was not raised in a conservative house. My father is a bit liberal for his age, and we always had books around and got into conversations together. I used to go to church when I was young, until I was seventeen or so. But now that I'm not formally practicing Christianity I wouldn't be able to tell what religion did for my character and personality; I don't know.

I believe that religion is between a person and his or her God. It shouldn't interfere in any government organization or be in any governmental system. Religion might provide some guidelines, for example when writing a constitution, but this is as far as you should go, in my opinion. I don't say that we should eliminate religion, and I feel that it's good to learn about different religions. It's also good to practice religion, but I believe it shouldn't affect one's choice of a leader. That choice should be based on the candidate's qualifications. If he is good, if he has new programs to introduce, I would never think of him in terms of religion.

I know that in America there are many evangelicals, but I do not believe in their idea that all the Jews must return to Palestine so Jesus Christ can come back from heaven. Maybe I haven't completed my homework on the Bible, but even if it mentioned this, I wouldn't believe it. It doesn't make a difference if Jews go back or not. That will never change the time that Christ will come; it won't make him come sooner or later.

Osama bin Laden has been classified as a terrorist. But he is a terrorist regardless of religion, a man who is out of time and place and history. Some people support him—I know this from the media, from taking taxis, and getting my hair cut, and talking to people in public places. I think it's because the Arab and Muslim worlds have no other public figure. They have no icon, no one to follow. And because people always need someone to follow, unfortunately it is now Osama by default.

I think I know why some people support him. It has to do with the standard of living in Arab, Third World, and Muslim countries. If a young man cannot get a job, doesn't have security, and has no future to plan for, then he will lean toward fanaticism to change his situation. Some people think, "If I can't live with dignity, then I might as well die for something." They try to be a martyr for God. This might explain why some people support bin Laden.

I think that some people try extreme ways to find meaning in life. Islamic history provides fertile soil for martyrdom in the name of jihad or in the name of God, against whatever evil Muslim people may be facing.

I would only sacrifice myself for my family, not for religion. But it is difficult to know how life experiences might change a person. Others might have different reasons for sacrificing themselves that they firmly believe in, but I know that I would give my life only for my family. Since I'm not married, I can't say if I would give my life for someone else.

*   *   *

I do not feel that I am anxious or worried, but sometimes I think, what if we woke up one day and learned that our president is dead? What type of government would we have then? I think about this occasionally, but it doesn't make me anxious all the time. When we had terrorist attacks on tourists here in Egypt I didn't stop going to the movies or change my way of life. You have to go on.

I consider myself fortunate, but also think about leaving Egypt, because I believe I can do better elsewhere. But I probably will not leave because of my family. My grandmother died recently, and that made me realize that being near family is important. I may change my mind in the future, but my parents are getting old and I do not want to leave them alone. I like my life in Egypt and I am fortunate to be educated, to have a nice job, a nice family, and nice friends. I do not know if I want to leave the Arab world yet.

*   *   *

When I was young I believed in Arab nationalism and still read some books on this subject. I love Hassanen Haikal, who believes in Arab nationalism. But I don't agree with him that all Arabs can become united and achieve something. That's not going to happen. But I do love the way he presents things and that he is optimistic.

The Arab world needs to change; it needs democracy. But not from America—I want the change to come from us, the people. Politics in Egypt went through a very steep decline since WWII. We used to have many effective political parties, and now we have corruption. I believe that one way of eliminating this corruption would be to have more effective political parties.

We also need to revisit our constitution. It says that we are a socialist country, but we are no longer, so this has to change. I hope to see these changes in my lifetime and would participate in making them happen if I could be assured that I would not end up in prison.

I do not like the way things are going right now because we are developing very slowly. We should have achieved more by now, but instead we are far behind and it's only getting worse. The way things are going we will get nowhere; we will not catch up with the rest of the world.

*   *   *

I do not believe that the majority of Americans are anti-Arab. I think the way they deal with us is strictly business. I read a lot about the neo-cons in the Republican administration right now. I know the biography of these people and about how George Bush got into the presidency and how he was targeting Iraq even before he became president. I read that he immediately targeted Iraq after September 11th and long before he invaded Afghanistan. What did they achieve in Afghanistan? There is nothing in Afghanistan and it's obvious what's going on: Afghanistan was business.

It's true that Saddam used to have one of the biggest organized armed forces in the Middle East, but that was ten or twelve years ago. Since the Gulf War in 1990 he no longer had such an army. The war on Iraq is about business, and because of this the neo-cons and some in the American administration do not necessarily represent the will of the American people—I feel it's important to differentiate between institutions and people.

For example, if the American administration decides to go to war with Egypt, I know there will be many Americans who will be against it. They will protest against a war with Egypt, because those in power don't necessarily represent the American people. I think the problem with the American people who support the war in Iraq is that they followed the media. They are very naïve if they only follow their media; the media will not tell them everything.

The American people don't know what's going on in the Middle East; maybe they don't know anything about the Middle East. Maybe they don't even care, and I wouldn't blame them if they do not. They live in the biggest economy and the strongest country in the world and maybe they do not want to know about other people in the world.

The problem with a democracy like America is that the media do not represent the people. If I said I knew why, I would be talking about conspiracy theories. Again, I believe it has to do with politics and business, and because the media is a business they are all very much connected. What I know about this comes from what I read, and you can never be certain that everything you read is factual.

I read that the Iraq War is an old project that goes back to the years after George Bush Sr. left the White House. His background, and that of Dick Cheney and Condoleeza Rice and others from that administration, is in the energy industry. I believe they had the plan to go into Iraq, but were waiting to get into power to act on it. This war in Iraq is not about securing the Middle East, and it's not about securing America; it's about securing one-third of the world's oil production. America is a very big consumer of oil.

While the current administration is in power I do not think that America will leave Iraq, because it won't be easy to leave. Even if George Bush is no longer in office America will not leave Iraq. Not because Iraq will end up in chaos, but because America is in too deep and can't just walk away. Perhaps with the help of the United Nations, a lot of financing, and a lot of other forces America will leave Iraq. I do not know much about John Kerry—I haven't learned enough about his ideas so I can't say what he would do. But I would definitely love to see someone other than George Bush as the American president.

When there is a presidential election in America the Arab world pays a lot of attention. Each time we wait to see if something will change in the way America handles the Middle East. But it never changes and will never change, so people are no longer optimistic.

Look at what happened to the poor captives in the Abu Ghraib prison in Iraq. It was disgusting. I would trade everything in the world to not be in those peoples' shoes. I thought about it and realized that this is a product of the America that we do not know about and we do not see. What do you expect from an 18-year-old American soldier who is assigned to such a place? He has no life experiences to compare it to! I believe this incident is one very bad example of the outcome of American culture.

Knowing about Abu Ghraib was bad enough, but seeing the pictures of the abuse was something else. I thought when I saw the pictures, "Not all Americans are doing this." Remember what I said about young Arabs—how they relate to fanatic groups? It's the same thing with these American soldiers and the prison. If they were normal people they wouldn't go in the army to earn more money or to get a scholarship.

Those soldiers who committed the abuse come from desperate environments, and such environments create a lot of complications. But not all Americans are like this, definitely not. I know it's a minority. I think those soldiers did what they did because they had no background information or knowledge about Arabs. Hollywood is in L.A., not in Cairo. Arabs know about America and Western culture from movies, but Americans don't know about us. The little they do see about us is bad and negative. We have exposure to other cultures, but they do not have exposure to us.

*   *   *

I hope that Americans do not re-elect George Bush. They need to realize that they are responsible for choosing an administration that's taking over the world. They have to think about this when they make their choice for president. Americans are introducing new education programs in the Arab world. They are starting to push for change in the constitutions of some Arab countries, but they will get nowhere. What I am afraid of is more attacks on America as a result of frustration with this administration. This administration is not intelligent enough to realize the frustration it is causing in the Arab world.

If there is one thing I want to do, it is to create a better picture of Arab people for Americans. I do not believe the American administration or Abu Ghraib abuse represents all of America. And I want this same principle to apply to Arabs; the actions of a few do not represent the sentiments of all.

This principle should apply everywhere. When I travel abroad I feel very small and realize that my knowledge is very minor. When I go to a place that I've never been before, like

England or China, I see how people live their lives. Just because I don't know anything about them doesn't make them bad.

I know that the Arab world is not in the best condition and hasn't been so for the past several years. So do not judge us just by what you see now, because there is so much you do not know about us. The Arab world is very much influenced by religion, culture, and history that you do not know much about. So do not rush to judge us; similarly we do not judge you with your wars and your prisoner torture.

Why do people judge other people without really knowing them?
Why do Americans judge us without knowing us or even visiting us?

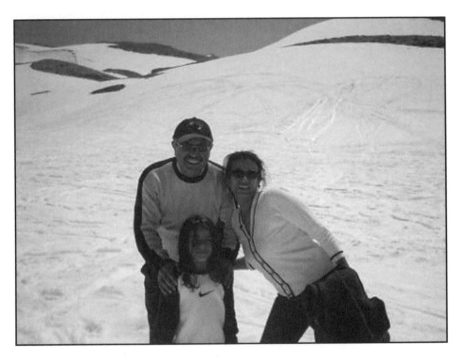

Hamed and his family playing in the snow

Hamed, 53
Construction Firm Owner/Manager
Kuwait
Muslim

I arrived in Michigan in 1973.... I watched the Watergate hearings all day, every day, and they really exposed me to U.S. politics. I still vividly remember senators Walker and Irvin questioning Attorney General John Mitchell, Haldeman, Erlichman, Dean, and the other top members of the Nixon administration who had engineered the burglary of the Democratic presidential campaign headquarters in the Watergate Hotel.

Introduction

I met Hamed at a birthday party in Kuwait. He walked in wearing traditional Kuwaiti dress, while his wife wore Western clothes. I told him about my project and he handed me his business card without any hesitation. I met him two days later at his office in an industrial area of Kuwait. As I was led to his office and offered strong Turkish coffee, a man came in. They hugged each other warmly and exchanged kisses on the cheek. This occurrence, so common in the Middle East, could be misunderstood if it took place somewhere else—say the streets of San Francisco. Hamed introduced me to the man and told him that I lived in the United States, but was born in Kuwait. This made the man extremely happy! I sensed that this visitor was a close friend of Hamed, and that my interview would have to wait until he left.

They spoke of things I didn't understand for thirty minutes and then the visitor left. Hamed explained that he worked with this man in the cattle business and explained to me in great detail the process of raising and selling cattle.

Once during the interview a non-Arab employee carrying several passports, probably belonging to laborers employed by Hamed, interrupted us to ask for extension of work permits. As soon as we finished the interview, Hamed rushed out of the office to greet with a hug and a kiss a woman wearing a traditional Kuwaiti long, black, loose outfit that did not cover her face. It turned out that she was Hamed's niece, ten years older than he!

She was a very interesting woman and I wanted to interview her too. I understood after meeting her why Hamed had such enlightened ideas: The whole family devoured books on a daily basis! As soon as his niece found out I was an Arab-American she wanted to talk about Hilary Clinton's book, which she was currently reading.

She said that "this strong woman" humiliated her husband in the book and, while he may have deserved it, he was the president of a very strong nation. She felt the book made American presidents look "not so strong," especially when a president is forced to sleep on the sofa. She wanted to know what Americans thought of this.

I told her that they had mixed feelings, depending on who you asked—a Democrat or a Republican. She did not like my answer and said, "I am not going to follow the news of American presidents if they behave in this embarrassing way while they run a super power." It amazed me how she spoke to me as an American, not as an Arab or Arab-American, and addressed me as "you" as in "you Americans."

Coming to my aid, Hamed told me not to be fooled by his niece's traditional costume. He said that she used to wear mini-skirts in the 1960s and '70s, and only began wearing traditional Kuwaiti dress after going on the Hajj (Pilgrimage to Mecca) a few years prior. She said that she felt more safe and free when wearing the long black outfit. "I can go anywhere dressed like this." Hamed and his niece spoke about the books they were reading and about the latest news. I wished I had a way to clearly transmit this surreal meeting to an American audience.

Meet Hamed

My name is Hamed. I grew up in Kuwait and finished high school there before attending the American University of Beirut in Lebanon in 1970. I studied pre-med there until 1973, when I felt that I needed to change my major. So I went to Ann Arbor, Michigan to complete my education.

Being a student at the American University in Beirut enriched my political consciousness about the Middle East and the entire world, and exposed me to people from all over the world including Americans. The political instability in Lebanon during that time was an eye-opening education for me.

Sometimes the university had to shut down for several months because of strikes and civil war, despite the fact that the full-scale Lebanese Civil War didn't erupt until 1975; I was in Michigan by then. But we experienced the early skirmishes of that war, and also a mini-civil war between the Lebanese army and the Palestinian commandoes. All of this contributed to my politicization, even though I was not a political science major. Seeing so many political events happen around you makes you pay a lot of attention to politics.

        *   *   *

I arrived in Michigan in 1973. I was too late for spring enrollment at the University of Michigan, so I decided to attend one summer semester at George Washington University, which is four blocks from the White House in Washington D.C, and then return to Michigan in the fall. What an impact that summer had on me! I took one math class in the evening and spent the rest of my day watching TV. I watched the Watergate hearings all day, every day, and they really exposed me to U.S. politics.

I still vividly remember senators Walker and Irvin questioning Attorney General John Mitchell, Haldeman, Erlichman, Dean, and the other top members of the Nixon administration who had engineered the burglary of the Democratic presidential campaign headquarters in the Watergate Hotel.

For me, fresh from the Middle East, it was a most shocking experience. To see ordinary people—congressmen, but still ordinary people—questioning the president's morality was something that would never happen in the Middle East. There, you must say complimentary things about your leaders and are not allowed, especially on TV, to criticize them. So you can only imagine what sort of impact watching the Watergate hearings live on TV had on me.[3]

This caused me to view the American political system with great respect. I always tell people here in the Middle East that, despite our criticism of the American political system, it is still a system that belongs to an open society that has the capacity to correct itself when it errs. We in the Arab world don't really have a political system, let alone a system that has the capacity to correct itself. The American system has the ability to evolve and develop through a feedback mechanism, which makes it able to correct itself.

*   *   *

---

[3] President Richard M. Nixon, elected to a second term in 1972, resigned in 1975 in the face of possible impeachment. The Watergate hearings went on for months, and it was suggested that Nixon and his aides knew about the burglary of Democratic Party national headquarters at the Watergate Hotel in Washington, DC. Amid the resulting scandal, Vice-President Spiro T. Agnew resigned. Nixon appointed Congressman Gerald R. Ford to fill the vice-president slot. Soon thereafter Nixon resigned and Ford became president. Ford then issued a "blanket pardon" to Nixon for any and all charges that might be brought against Nixon in connection with the Watergate burglary. Several Nixon aides went to prison.

I was not a typical engineering student in the U.S.; I was very active in the organization of Arab students. Shortly after I arrived in the U.S. and began studying at the University of Michigan that fall, the October 1973 war between Egypt, Syria, and Israel broke out. We followed it closely, and it added to or exasperated our political consciousness.

I stayed in Ann Arbor for four years, much longer than I should have. I think my political activities and campus involvement delayed my graduation, and this made my family angry. But I am now fifty-three years old and run my own company, and I feel that the delay in my graduation was beneficial to my emotional and intellectual development.

I feel that my experiences as a student contributed to my political maturation. For example, I react much more slowly than I used to, and feel more mature and patient. I meet people who are college-educated and even some who have doctoral degrees, but they still react to certain things like children. So I think that every stage in your life, no matter how problematic it is, has its benefits.

*   *   *

Currently, I am a partner and the manager of a construction company which employs about 250 people. We specialize in industrial flooring; our main operations are finishing work, painting, waterproofing, concrete repair, and decorative finishing.

I was married in 1987 and have four children now aged six, twelve, fifteen, and sixteen. I try to take them to school every day, because it is an opportunity for me to interact with them, to listen to their complaints, and to learn from them. They attend a bilingual English school, but I am worried about their ability to read and write in Arabic so I watch them closely.

I think that we have an educational problem in Kuwait. The English curriculum of the school is very attractive; the English textbooks are much more attractive than the Arabic ones, so students prefer the English subjects. The students find the Arabic books boring—not because of the Arabic language, but because the

Ministry of Education is not hiring qualified personnel to create more appealing Arabic books. I know that my kids do not put extra effort into learning the Arabic language, so I speak with them in Arabic. I have reservations about people who talk to their children only in English; I would like Arab children to be fluent in both languages.

       *   *   *

I do not feel particularly vulnerable or unsafe when I leave my house every morning. I feel very lucky to be living in Kuwait, and I am even building another house here. I think that Kuwaitis in general are better off than their neighbors; they are lucky, but not necessarily happy. They are lucky because they live in a political oasis compared to the neighboring radical countries of Iran and Saudi Arabia and the war and instability in Iraq. But I feel that Kuwait needs to change, even though we are economically better off, because there are so many weaknesses in our political and economic systems.

Kuwait needs some change, but I think there will not be major or drastic change here without similar changes in Saudi Arabia, Iran, and Iraq. I'm very hopeful—in spite of the suffering of the Iraqis, the war, and the instability—that in the future Iraq will be stable and prosperous. I don't expect Iraq to reach the same economic level as Kuwait, but I do believe Iraqi society has the potential and the ability to be productive and spread principles of freedom in the Middle East.

Economically, we can start making changes now. The Kuwaiti population is about 800,000. We are surrounded by several poor Arab and Asian countries, and because there is no minimum wage in Kuwait we can recruit low-wage labor from India, Pakistan, and all over the Arab world. The laborers are happy with their meager wages, but this contributes to the low productivity of Kuwaitis. I will give you an example.

If my house needed simple repairs and I lived in Europe or the U.S., I would do it myself to save money. But in Kuwait this same repair job will cost me two dinars, or about six American dollars. So, why should I waste an hour of my time to fix it? I have cheap labor everywhere that I can get any time I want. But this makes me feel less creative and I do not develop new skills. Also, my kids will have the same attitude when they grow up and so will the whole country.

Politically, I know that the ruling family is legitimate because the people chose it, but even members of the ruling family realize that Kuwait requires the kind of political change that will not require the Prime Minister to be from the ruling family. In the long run, I wish for Kuwait to be a constitutional monarchy. I don't think the people are ready to accept a Prime Minister from outside the ruling family—they believe that an "ordinary" man would not have enough power and legitimacy to make major decisions. But I also believe that this could change in the future; many members of the ruling family are convinced that eventually that family must cede power to the people.

I know that people might find it strange that I support a monarchy while also being very much against monarchs accumulating wealth and leaving their subjects poor. Nobody can accept that, but the historical development of the Gulf States and Saudi Arabia is very unique and unprecedented. Let's look at Kuwait as a case study. Its population in 1950 was no more than 50,000 people—it was not even a city then; it was a town where four years earlier the first oil field had been discovered. Before the discovery of oil, Kuwait had a subsistence economy; people hardly had sufficient food to eat. The ruling family taxed the people— mainly the merchant class—to generate revenue. But in four short years, the economy of Kuwait developed rapidly. All of the monarchs, or Amirs (princes), of the Gulf states suddenly found themselves in control of the oil and its wealth.

What they did with this new wealth varied from state to state. Kuwait handled its new money more wisely than others, but I wouldn't say it was spent 100% wisely. With sudden wealth people get greedy, whether they are of the ruling family or ordinary people; this is human nature. The merchant class, for example, benefited the most from the oil boom because the government bought land from them at very high prices. This new wealth turned them from a simple merchant class to a sophisticated one that specialized in franchising European and American brand names.

The oil revenue in Kuwait was spent mainly to employ the people. Many are critical of that economic decision, but I would say that the ruler then had very few choices—the only way to improve the peoples' situation was to pay them salaries and find them jobs. Jobs did not mean that employees had to be productive. All that mattered was that they were formally on the payroll. I would say most of the money went to paying salaries for unproductive labor, which continues today.

Of course there is always a better alternative, but I cannot blame the ruler or the government for choosing this option; it was easy, but it was also reasonable. Kuwait did some thing good in creating a health care system and offering free education to all citizens. Kuwait was, in a way, a pioneer in modernizing and transforming a traditional tribal society into a modern one.

Despite the problems Kuwaiti society suffers from, I would say that we have one of the best living standards in the Gulf area. Not many neighboring countries have managed to achieve what Kuwait has. This may have to do with the nature of the ruling families of other Gulf states.

Kuwait was able to liberalize politically and adopted a formal constitution in 1961; by 1963 we had an elected parliament. So Kuwaiti citizens have some say in how their country is run, especially compared to the Saudis. I wouldn't say this ruling family is better or worse than the other, but it is a completely different political and historical experience. The ruling family in Saudi Arabia believes that they created the Kingdom; without them, the state is not legitimate. It is a different experience altogether in Kuwait.

The ruling family in Kuwait was chosen in the late 18th century. The merchant families of Kuwait traveled in Asia and India, and this exposed them to other cultures and peoples. Also, the geographic location of Kuwait helped it to be more open to the world. In Arabia things were different because the Saud family conquered the country and united the vast area of modern day Saudi Arabia under their rule. This made them very powerful, but I think it has reached a stage where it will backfire. Saudi Arabia now faces a real dilemma: how to change and become a modern country.

Democracy should not have an identity and a nationality. It is an effective political system which evolved through time because it proved to benefit the people, whether it's in Turkey or the United States or Germany or Israel. One should not think of democracy as an exclusively Western model or concept, because that would be a very limiting definition that fits only Westerners. I don't believe this; I think that a democratic system is appropriate for all societies.

I don't expect a Western-style democracy to be implemented in our area. What we will eventually do is create a democratic political system of our own that is similar to the democracies of Europe, the United States, and Japan, but still distinctly Arabic.

*   *   *

I don't think Americans are born anti-Arab. The media contributes to bias against Arabs, but I think we bear some responsibility as well. I think September 11th contributed greatly to American anti-Arab sentiments, but we should not blame Americans. We should blame ourselves. I don't think we Arabs have introduced ourselves to the world in the right way, and I think that we have to admit when we are wrong. We should not become nationalists or over-sensitive in covering our mistakes; and we have made many mistakes.

*   *   *

It is very easy to become a fundamentalist. You subdue your emotions and feel that you are legitimate before the people and before God. To be a liberal, you have to put forth effort. You have to read, travel, become educated; it is a lot of work. But all a fundamentalist needs to do is go to a mosque all the time. People here don't go to libraries. It's not acceptable to go to a library to spend time reading, but it is normal to go to a mosque five times a day. You can be socially accepted because you are religious. But if you only read the Quran and do not receive a proper education or learn the ability to interpret a highly literal text there is a possibility that you will misinterpret things and turn into a fanatic. This happens to many people when they try to interpret reality based on religion, whether they are Christian, Jewish, or Muslim. They turn into radicals.

Islamic fanaticism starts with an inherent animosity towards the West due to its unconditional support of Israel. But the bin Laden phenomenon is part of the strategic political mistake the United States made when it supported Muslim fundamentalists against the Afghani Marxist regime in Kabul. Many American academics and journalists admit that at least the Marxists belonged to a Western culture, and there was a chance to communicate with them and eventually negotiate with them. But when you compound the problem with differing religions the situation becomes difficult to deal with. The U.S. and Saudi Arabian support of political fundamentalism and regimes has backfired on both.

I read in the news that a Palestinian assistant to al Zarqawi in Iraq was killed. Some Palestinians are radicals, but historically they are not really religious radicals; they are leftists, Marxists, or belong to secular organizations. To have a Palestinian who is a religious fundamentalist is new; it is something that we have encountered only in the last twenty years, and I would not be surprised to read that this guy who was killed recently in Fallujah was educated in a religious university in Saudi Arabia.

A lot of oil money was spent to radicalize the Saudi people—not intentionally, but it was a Saudi government policy to allow these people to grow, to provide them with economic tools to open schools and confine education to a religion. The reasoning was to occupy the young with religion so they would not have a chance to think about political change. But it comes back to what I said before: If you confine education to religion you will turn students into radicals.

There is hope for change, but it will not happen in one year or two years; it takes decades to change people. I think we have to modify religious education and learn more about other religions. Recently, I participated in a meeting with a professor from Kuwait University. We discussed this point and reached the conclusion that there is a lack of teaching of comparative religions in the Arab world, not only in Kuwait.

The problem with Muslim fundamentalists is that they think that history started only after Muhammad (peace be upon him[4])—that before the Prophet Muhammad (PBUH) there was no history. They read about all the previous prophets only in the Quran. They look at the Quran as the source of history, yet millions of Muslims see it as a book of science and logic—not just a religious book or a divine book. So there is a structural problem in teaching religion in some Arab countries.

*   *   *

The events of September 11th remind me of a verse in the Quran, 2:216, which says, "But it is possible that ye dislike a thing which is good for you, And that ye love a thing which is bad for you But Allah (God) knoweth, And ye know not." I think September 11th changed the attitude of the decision-makers in the U.S. In spite of all the pain, I think that in the long run it will have some benefits. The immediate benefit is that the U.S. government realized that for decades it had allied itself with dictators and that the major players in September 11th were Saudi Arabian and

---

[4] "Peace be upon him" and its abbreviated form, "PBUH," denote a special blessing of the particular prophet named. As a sign of respect, Muslims add "peace be upon him" after the name of prophets when spoken and "PBUH" when written.

Egyptian—countries that were supposed to be American allies. Something must be wrong.

The U.S. asked itself, "How can I be an ally of a country whose people hate me?" There must be something wrong. What is wrong is the fact that the U.S. is supporting unfair and unjust political systems in these countries, so their people develop animosity against the U.S. Most experts believe that a major change in the Arab world will require that the U.S. put pressure on governments in the area to give more rights to the people.

*   *   *

Then we come to the situation in Iraq. Most Arabs are very much against U.S. interference in Iraq. I am not; I am very much in favor of what the U.S. has done. I have to admit that it was mismanaged; the Americans were not prepared for the day after the regime fell. But I am not against the principle of invading Iraq to topple Saddam Hussein's regime. However, this does not mean that I will support everything the U.S. does in the area.

When I talk to my friends in Lebanon, Palestine, and the entire Arab world who are against U.S. interference in Iraq, I tell them that I have developed a conviction that we should not automatically be anti-U.S. toward everything it does. If the U.S says a regime is bad, we should not say it is good just to spite the U.S.

I am very much against the U.S. policy on Palestine. I feel that the U.S. government and the American people are losing a lot because of their support of Israel. This is a major cause of the Arab people developing animosity toward the U.S. In fact, it is the number one cause of this animosity and something must be done about it. But on the other hand, while I reject the American attitude toward Palestine, I am very much in favor of the American policy in Iraq, even though I have some reservations about the details of the strategy.

I don't think the U.S. will pull its troops out of Iraq. They cannot afford to do so, because that might result in an Iraqi civil war. I also do not wish to see a theocracy in Iraq; that would be a change to something worse.

              *   *   *

For fifty years, we have watched the U.S. and the West support Israel against the Arabs—especially so in the last four years, during which the Israeli regime has received unprecedented support from the U.S. This has really antagonized the Arab people. The American policy with Israel has been radicalizing Israeli society, pushing it towards the right. I think the U.S. should play a more moderate role for the sake of both Palestine and Israel.

It's interesting that, had I been born a European, I would still support the Palestinians because I would have been a socialist European, or maybe a social democrat European. I would still sympathize with the Palestinians, because from reading the history of Zionism and the Palestinian question, I realize that the Palestinians received an unfair deal from everyone—from the Arabs, the Europeans, and the Zionists. The Arabs promised them support and did not deliver, and the Europeans and Americans provided too much support to the Israelis.

The roots of Palestinian agony are really related to the suffering of the Jews at the hands of Europeans. It is the European Christians, not the Palestinians, who persecuted the Jews, yet it is the Palestinians who have to pay the price. The first meeting of Zionists took place in Basel, Switzerland in 1870; Zionism is much older than the state of Israel.

One should ask: Why was the political idea of Zionism created? Zionism was formed as a mechanism to listen to the suffering Jews. The Jews suffered in Europe throughout history and then more harshly under the Nazis. I think without the suffering of the Jews under the Nazi regime and without the Holocaust, Israel would not have been established. And that is why I am very much against denying the Holocaust.

I don't respect people who deny the Holocaust. It's not a question of numbers, of whether Nazis killed ten thousand Jews or one million Jews. It is all a crime, and it is not an ordinary crime to kill people who are innocent and who have contributed to the enrichment of European culture. The Europeans took fellow Europeans who had enriched their homelands and made them suffer. I think there is a direct association between the Holocaust and the establishment of the state of Israel. So Israel really started as a European problem that was then exported to the Middle East. They shoved their problem that they created down our throats.

Jews in Palestine in the twentieth century just before the creation of the state of Israel made up no more than seven percent of the total population. Based on this fact and the histories of the Zionist movement and our area, I would say that the Palestinians received a very unfair deal. What did the world expect them to do—sit and watch their land being taken away from them? Americans would have fought back, too.

This problem can be solved by putting more pressure on the Israeli government to withdraw from all or most of the occupied West Bank and giving Palestinians the chance to form their own state. I think that over time these two states will become one. Animosity generates more animosity, hatred generates more hatred, but peace will generate less hatred and more love. I would not be surprised if, in 100 years, Israel and Palestine are one state.

But until this happens, Arabs can live with an Israeli state and a Palestinian state. However, I think the U.S. should get more involved in Israeli politics, play a more active role in supporting the political parties in Israel who are moderate and willing to give a better deal to the Palestinians.

*   *   *

Americans often say they know what Muslims are willing to die for, but not what they are willing to live for. I am not willing to die for any cause; I lost the stamina to die for a cause a long time ago. What I live for now is my family and my friends. I'm enjoying life. I enjoy traveling, food, reading, and writing. I enjoy my life with my wife.

*   *   *

I know the popular U.S. concept is that Arab men see women as objects, but I don't think you can generalize that all Arab men see women as objects. I think this is a stigma which is very wrong. I think Arabs have problems in admitting the strength of a woman; most Arab men are afraid of the strength of their women. True, women in some Arab countries do not vote and some cover their hair with the *hijab,* but they are very strong women. When an Arab woman covers her hair it does not mean that she is weak. She chose to cover her hair—it is a personal choice and she should have the freedom to choose how she wants to dress. *The hijab* does not mean that a woman is weak.

I know Saudi Arabian women who are veiled, but they clearly run their households. Arab men are in a way very romantic and afraid of women leaving them. That is why they accept freedom for themselves, but not for their women; they think that when there is more freedom there is a greater chance that their women will leave them. An Arab man would be devastated if his wife fell in love with another man.

There is a book by a female Moroccan sociologist, Fatima Marnisi, who wrote extensively about the issue of *al Hishma* (dressing and behaving modestly). Look at you, for example. You are wearing Western clothing with no hair cover, yet you look modest—more so than some women and girls who cover their hair. You are not wearing too much makeup like they do.

I once wrote a column on this issue and argued that the purpose of religion is not to make you cover or uncover, but to make all of us behave and dress modestly—with *hishma*, as we say it in the Arab world. The problem with some of our interpreters of religion is that they blame women for everything and say that it is the dress of the woman that makes men sin. Well, it is also the sin of man, and it is his problem if he can't think in a decent way when he sees a woman. What is interesting is that when I write on such issues I do not get negative feedback from readers.

Of course I write in Arabic; it is the language that makes me love being an Arab. We also have very strong family relations—a bit too strong sometimes. We need to find a balance between the two extremes of Western and Arab family life.

*   *   *

There is a difference between what I like and what I respect about America. I respect the discipline, hard work, and freedom; the freedom of individuals to make major decisions concerning their lives. A personal decision regarding education or marriage is a freedom that our strong Arab family ties prevent us from making, and I feel that is wrong.

Once or twice an American has asked me if I have heard of Jesus Christ. Once while I was in the U.S. with a Palestinian student an American lady asked him what his religion was; he said Christian. The lady then asked him who had converted him, and he replied, "Jesus Christ and his apostles." Jesus Christ (peace be upon him) is from our area; he belonged to us before he belonged to Western culture.

Many Americans do not know that, as a Muslim, I have to know about Jesus Christ, and that there are dozens of verses about him in the Quran. I do not think that Americans know that Jesus is mentioned in the Quran more than our Prophet Muhammad (PBUH), or that there is a whole chapter named after his virgin mother, an honor not bestowed on any Muslim woman.

The Prophet Muhammad (PBUH) married a Christian woman and maintained good relations with his contemporary Christians of Mecca and Medina. We Muslims do not feel awkward or upset if the name of Jesus is invoked, because he is one of the prophets and we revere them all. We should always learn from Jesus Christ.

I just got back from a trip to Saudi Arabia where I noticed that my niece, a teacher, had an ornamented ceramic tile with Arabic writing that says: "If a man say I love God and hate his brother, he is a liar." I told her it was a beautiful phrase and asked who said it. She told me, "Jesus Christ, peace be upon him."

You are an American, but you are an Arab-American, so my question to you will be different from one I pose to an American who lives in Lincoln, Nebraska or San Francisco, or one who lives on the East Coast, or one who teaches at Columbia University or is a farmer in Iowa. But, in general, I think Americans are hardworking people, and because of this they are good people.

I lived in America and I have many American friends, and I would like to ask each American a different question. I cannot just ask one question of all Americans; they are not all the same.

Hassan at work in the salon

Hassan, 24
Hair Stylist
Amman, Jordan
Muslim

I would like Americans to know that not all Muslims wish the U.S. harm. Millions of Muslims live in peace and are not jealous of America. I am proud of being an Arab...I am happy with my life. I am not jealous of anyone.

Introduction

Appearance is important even when you are carrying a tape recorder, getting in and out of taxis, and asking strangers very political questions. Shortly after I arrived in Amman I realized I needed to get my hair styled, so my friend Dina took me to a beauty salon less than a mile from the highly-fortified American embassy.

The salon was very busy, full of female customers and male stylists. The receptionist was a twenty-four-year-old Jordanian desperate to go to the United States. When he found out I was American and writing a book he clung to me, thinking that I had influence with the U.S. State Department.

The salon had several young male employees. Some washed hair and massaged scalps and one young Egyptian man walked through the salon offering clients soft drinks, hot tea, or coffee. I requested a coffee and sipped it while I waited—it was the best Arabic coffee I had ever tasted.

I was soon greeted by the stylist who would be attending to me. His name was Hassan and he seemed very young. "Thank God I am only getting my hair set, not cut," I thought to myself as

I followed him to his station. "He is too young to know how to cut hair!"

I am usually very quiet while I get my hair done. Sometimes I read, but most often I just like to observe others. Watching the activity in a salon is like having several soap operas running simultaneously in front of you. One can easily write a novel just on the things you see and hear. All sorts of people walk in; old and young, fat and thin, short and tall, rich and poor, Arab and foreign, professionals and housewives. As I sat down in Hassan's chair, I even noticed the winner of the first *Star Academy of the Arab World* television show leaving the salon.

Seeing the "star" brought out my reporter instincts and I started asking Hassan questions. My first question was a bit too forward: Do you want to move to the U.S. and live there?

Hassan stopped and looked at me in the mirror. "No, why should I leave?"

I explained why I was asking and described my project. I then asked if he would like to be in my book and he said he would.

I arranged to meet him a few days later after he finished work. He seemed like a very sincere and kind person with raw innocence and frankness. He was not afraid to show his emotions, and I was sad when he began to cry at the end of our interview.

Meet Hassan

My name is Hassan. I was born in Jordan in 1980 and studied at a Roman Catholic School. I went to college to become a hairdresser and now work at a beauty salon in Amman. I have wonderful parents and three sisters. Two of my sisters are married; the youngest is sixteen years old and still single. My father is an engineer and my mother is a teacher.

It was not easy for me to become a hairstylist. My family tried to convince me to enroll at a university and get a regular degree. My father was willing to send me anywhere in the world if I would study something other than hairstyling. He even offered me a brand new car if I would go to the university. But studying was never my passion; in fact, I finished high school just to please my family. I entered college for their sake, but in the end I chose what I wanted.

My passion for hairstyling started when I was very young. Even when I was 10 years old and people would ask me what I wanted to be when I grew up I would say, "A hair stylist." I started to think seriously about it when I was twelve. I went to a salon with my sister on the night of her wedding and watched the stylists work. I was fascinated.

I started to ask people about the job and its advantages and disadvantages. Everything I learned made me like the profession more and I told my family that hairstyling was the profession I wanted to pursue.

*   *   *

My father was born in Anabta, Palestine in 1948, and my mother in Jordan in 1955. Both of my parents completed high school in Jordan; my father fled from Palestine with his family when the Israeli occupation began. My mother went to college in Amman while my dad studied engineering in the United States. He left the U.S. as soon as he finished his studies to work in the Gulf region—Saudi Arabia, the United Arab Emirates, and Kuwait. He also worked in the Far East, Athens, and Greece, and he is now working in Amman.

My original nationality is Palestinian, but I have a Jordanian passport and citizenship. I was born in Jordan and have lived here all my life; this is where I studied and where I work. I know everything about Jordan and King Hussein. I have never met him, but I feel like I know him personally, because he was always in our schoolbooks, on TV, and in magazines.

I feel like a Jordanian of Palestinian origin, but I would not return to Palestine. I feel that Palestine belongs to those who fight for it, not those who live elsewhere and doing nothing for it. I feel that I have not earned the right to return to Palestine.

*   *   *

When asked where I am from I always respond, "Jordan." People do not usually ask about my religion, but when they do I tell them I am Muslim. For me, religion is personal. I fear God and try to live by his laws, but that's it. I never introduce myself as Muslim, only as Jordanian or Arab.

Many Arabs do not mention their religion, even Christians. I know this from my school days and Christian friends. We used to have church at school and were separated during religion class. Muslim students went to one room and Christian students to another, and when religion class was over we'd go back to our normal classes and study together. We were and still are friends, and never debated religious issues or quarreled about them. I believe that we all should live in harmony together with full and equal rights.

I do not have a problem working with people of other religions. I feel that everyone has his or her personal life, and religion is something personal. I think that I have read the Bible more than the Quran; I still have a copy of the Bible at home that I read from time to time. A few months ago I went to the movies and watched the film *The Passion of the Christ* and as soon as I got home I read the Bible to learn more about the last twelve hours of Jesus Christ, peace be upon Him. He is one of the prophets that we believe in, and I do not feel that reading the Bible can influence my Muslim faith.

As a Muslim, I am most proud of my language and the Holy Quran. I can read the Bible in Arabic, but an American cannot read the Quran. He can read a translation of the *meaning* of the Quran, but it will not be the same as the Quran as revealed in Arabic.

*   *   *

My family is what makes me most proud to be an Arab. I was the only son and brother in my family, and this is important to an Arab family—I am the one who will take care of my parents when they are older and help my sisters if they need it. The family unit is the most important thing in an Arab's life. This is why I never think of leaving Jordan. Although my parents would not mind if I left, I cannot do that to them. Maybe when I retire or have achieved my career goals I will go to Hawaii or to England.

I feel that I am 100% free here; free to write or say whatever I want without anyone interfering. Sometimes an American will ask, "I know what you are ready to die for, but what are you living for?" I do not think that he or she knows what I would live or die for. I want to live for many reasons; to enjoy my life and build my future. I want to work, make a decent living for myself, and have a family. I do not want to die for any reason.

I would never kill myself to be a martyr for God. Life and death are destined by God. Besides, if my country was attacked I could defend her in many different ways: I could write an article in the newspaper or design signs. I love life and want to live.

*   *   *

I think Osama bin Laden is a silly person. We never benefited from him as Palestinians, Jordanians, Arabs, or Muslims. Muslims have a goal that Palestine and Jerusalem be freed. But bin Laden did not help Muslims obtain their goal of a free Jerusalem. He just killed innocent people. If he is a patriot and loves Islam then let him reveal himself and come out and talk to the world. I personally do not like him at all.

If I were the American president I would not have attacked the Afghanis and Taliban after September 11th. Osama bin Laden is Saudi, so why didn't the U.S. president attack Saudi Arabia? I wouldn't attack Afghanistan even if bin Laden lived there. The Afghani people did not attack the Americans, yet they are the ones who died in the war. A president should be 100% certain that Afghanistan attacked the U.S. before launching a war. The American president has the best intelligence in the world and his agencies could prove if Afghani people had anything to do with

September 11th. So many innocent civilians died, and where is Osama now? Making videos!

After September 11th many Americans wondered why they were attacked. The administration's explanation was that Arabs are jealous of the U.S. and democracy, so they attacked. But not all Muslims attacked America; only 19 of the 1.5 billion Muslims in the world attacked. The people who did it were not jealous of Americans—they were upset at American foreign policy, the fact that the U.S. controls Saudi oil fields, the Israeli occupation of Palestine, and the killing of Iraqis by economic sanctions.

I am not even sure if Osama bin Laden was behind September 11th. But I would like Americans to know that not all Muslims wish the U.S. harm. Millions of Muslims live in peace and are not jealous of America. I am proud of being an Arab because of the life I live in the Arab world, especially in Jordan. I am happy with my life. I am not jealous of anyone.

On the other hand, I think many Americans hate Arabs. What the government does influences the people; it can make people either love or hate the Arabs. I encourage Americans to visit Arab countries, to see how people there live and find out that not all Arabs live the same way or even look the same. We think in so many different ways that one cannot say 350 million people are the same. Americans might also find out that some Arabs are happier than Americans. The true picture of Arabs should be given to Americans so they will know our reality.

The American government and media should show people the true picture of Arab society. We are not sitting around watching the Americans and waiting to criticize them. Many of us live happily and are content with our lives.

*   *   *

The media reported that America invaded Iraq to look for weapons of mass destruction, but I do not think that was the main reason. It was the wealth of Iraq that they sought—and a foothold in the region. America can destroy Iraq with its weapons, but it did not; it invaded the country to stay there.

I am not sure if American troops will withdraw from Iraq. They might pretend to withdraw just for show, but the leadership put in place will stay and represent the American will. It is very annoying to see people being killed every day just because they are defending their country. It is hard to imagine myself living that way. If I lived in Palestine or Iraq and my brothers were killed, what would I do? I am not in this situation, but I feel the pain of those that are; it impacts me emotionally.

I do not think that the situation in the Arab world should be changed primarily by outsiders. The Americans have come to change us, but we don't need this. The only thing that needs to change is those who harm and kill others. All people dream of and work for a better future. They should be helped, not changed.

We do need democracy, but one that we develop on our own—not one decided for us by others. It is difficult to attain democracy because we are used to things as they are, but we must have free elections. I do not want the president to stay in power for thirty-five years. As an Arab citizen, I would like that to change.

I do not think that only a few people will be able to make this change; maybe as a nation we can. There are many people in power who have much to lose if change sweeps the Arab world, so they will do everything in their power to prevent change from happening. Perhaps if all the people of one country went on a strike, they could bring about change, or force those in power to change things. Honestly, I do not think that the Arab world will change much in the next 100 years.

If we used more technology, then people from across the world could change things together. Maybe the Internet will help us change things. The Internet is such a powerful tool; it can bring people together even though they are great distances apart. For example, I met an Australian through the Internet. We chatted for seven months and then he decided to visit me in Jordan. He came and stayed here for three weeks and visited historical places like

Jerash and Petra. We got along very well and went out every day and never talked politics. All I wanted to do was to take care of my guest and make sure he was having a good time.

He told me that he never expected Amman to be so beautiful. He thought Amman was a village with trash in the streets! He expected to find dirty hotels, but was surprised by how clean Amman was. I took him many places—Aqaba, Petra, Mount Nebo, the Dead Sea, the place where Jesus Christ was baptized. He liked them all and was surprised that Muslims have always maintained and protected Christian places.

So you see how technology made an Australian fall in love with Jordan and like Arabs. Maybe it will also make Americans change their minds about us. If they visit with us or chat with us on the Internet they will realize that we are not criminals, that we do not kill ourselves for nothing.

Arabs do not hate Americans. It is possible that we like some of what they have, but it is not jealousy or hatred. I would like to be able to protest like they do when they do not like something their government is doing, but I do not hate them because they protest! I do not know anyone who has said something bad about the American people. Some might criticize the American government, but not the people. Actually, we feel sorry for the American people because they have nothing to do with all the bad things that their government does.

I had a friend who was killed because he was an Arab and a Muslim. Why did they kill him? Because he was Muslim? I would like to know why Americans fear Muslims. Why didn't my friend's killers talk to him first and find out if he supported September 11th? I still cry when I think about him.

There is one question that I have always wanted to ask Americans, and that is, "Why did some Americans kill ordinary Muslims after September 11th?"

Ola at work as an attorney in Amman, Jordan

Ola, 44
Attorney
Amman, Jordan
Muslim

As an Arab lawyer who likes the American people I would like to tell the American president that he needs to treat us the way he treats Americans...as we all condemned the criminal actions of September 11th and the death of innocent people, we ask the Americans to condemn the killing of Iraqis and Palestinians.

Introduction

I arranged to meet Ola at noon at her office in Amman, Jordan, which was 15 minutes away by car. Several of my relatives offered to let me use their cars or to drive me themselves while I was in Amman, but I declined their generous offers. I wanted to take as many taxis as possible so I could talk to the drivers.

I asked most drivers some of the questions that Americans had posed, and the resulting conversations were always interesting. I enjoyed the surprise on one young driver's face, whom I will call Amer, when I asked if he would like to live in the U.S. Amer was smoking and listening to very loud Arabic pop music. My question startled him; he put his cigarette out, turned the music down, looked at me in the mirror, and said, "WHAT?"

I smiled and repeated the question, but Amer still just stared—I think he was trying to figure me out. He asked, "Are you from there?" I said, "I am an Arab-American, and I speak publicly about Arab people and Islam. I like to talk to Arabs to see how they think. He opened up and said, "No, I would not go to the, U.S., no way." My heart sank as I began to wonder if maybe most Arabs hated the U.S. after all.

I asked Amer why, and his answer left me wondering whether to laugh or cry. He said he could not go to the U.S. because he didn't know how to speak English. He told me that he had tremendous self-respect and felt that if he went to America without knowing how to speak English, Americans would make fun of him. He said he would die before he allowed this to happen. So it was only English that was stopping him from leaving his family and moving to the U.S. It wasn't politics, religion, September 11th, the war in Afghanistan, Iraq, or the Patriot Act that made him stay in Jordan; it was a language barrier!

Amer told me that he earned five Jordanian Dinars a day (less than $12) and spends two on cigarettes and the rest on his mother and two younger brothers, whom he supported.

"How do you think I feel," he asked me, "as the man of the house when my youngest brother is gravely ill and I have not one penny to take him to the doctor? I cannot look into my mom's eyes because I see her pain for my brother and for my inability to do anything for him. How can I get married? I am thirty-three years old and I cannot get married and I do not think that I will ever be able to. Yes, if I could learn English I would go to America and work day and night and make a decent living and send all my money to my mom and brother."

We got lost and found ourselves across from the old intelligence building in Amman, which was once called by many people the Palestine Hotel. The government department was moved to a new location long ago, but I seized the moment to ask Amer some political questions. I was very surprised that he did not hesitate to answer me. He told me that he was very upset at what was happening in Iraq and Palestine and in the rest of the Arab world, but poor people like him did not think of doing something about it.

He pointed to the fancy European and Japanese cars and SUVs around us and said, "These people can afford to protest and ask for change, but many are corrupt and they are benefiting from all this."

When we reached my destination he refused to take money from me, but I swore on his mother's soul and well-being that he must allow me to pay him. By the time I met Ola I was depressed, but she gave me hope.

Meet Ola

I come from a Jordanian family whose roots can be traced to Damascus. My family is religiously conservative, but not in a domineering way. We grew up seeing our father praying five times a day and fasting regularly, and we studied at an Islamic school. But we had total freedom in everything—our clothes, appearance, studies, and choice of husband. My sisters and I enjoyed personal freedom up to the point that no one interfered even when we decided to wear a hair cover; it was simply our choice. My sisters and I grew up feeling that we had the power to make decisions, but also that we should take responsibility for those decisions. Although we grew up in a traditional house, I felt that I was like any other female student in Amman.

All my life I dreamed of becoming a lawyer, and luckily the law school at Jordan University had just opened its doors when I graduated from high school. This was in 1987, and at that time I was reluctant to study law because there were only about three or four female lawyers in Jordan; I was very hesitant about joining the profession. But my father and mother encouraged me and said that it was good for me, so I entered law school and graduated in 1992.

I could not do the two years training required by graduate law students because I was under the minimum age. Instead, I worked for one year at the Income Tax Department. After that I had enough ambition to aim for a Master's degree, so I quit my job and became a full-time student.

After I finished my Master's, I married a former colleague and had three children. I did not work for five years, but in 1990 when my son went to school I started my law training. Since I already held a Master's I only had to complete one year of training, which I completed at a private law firm in 1991. I loved my firm and its reputation and work ethics, and was happy when they asked me to stay on after finishing my training. I worked there for nine years before I became a full partner.

When I started my law training I was not particularly religious and did not wear a hair cover. Later on I became more committed to religion, thank God, and decided to cover my hair. My partner, Adeeb, has been a lawyer since 1972 and is a Christian Arab. I do not think he thought about my decision to cover my hair for more than twenty-four hours. If he was reluctant about it, it was not for personal reasons, but because he was worried that clients may react negatively. But all of our clients knew me very well and were not surprised; I think they may even have felt that I was becoming more committed to living Islam. Adeeb and I have great debates and discussions about all kinds of issues including religion, and we sometimes argue with each other, but we have a great working relationship.

Our law firm deals mainly with two types of cases, commercial and civil, which make up 70% of the cases we handle. The other 30% of cases deal with church law and Christian divorce.

Divorce for Christians in Jordan takes place at Christian courts where the judges are priests. It does not take place in regular civil courts, as it does for Muslims. I attend the court and work with priests, who never object to the fact that a Muslim is handling a Christian divorce case. I think we deal with so many Christian divorce cases because my partner is Christian and knows a lot about the various Christian sects in Jordan. We have several Christian sects and each has its own court. If one goes to the wrong court, he or she will be in trouble and face problems.

My role is to represent either the husband or the wife and to present the case in front of the judges. No one has ever protested against my presence in the court. There is a big difference between conducting a Muslim divorce and a Christian one. We have only one court for Muslims, because we have only one sect of Muslims in Jordan—the Sunnis. There are different locations where these courts exist, but they all follow one law: the Jordanian Personal Status Law that is derived from Islamic Law (Sharia). In Islam, we have three stages for divorce. First is the revocable divorce, which must be registered at the court by the party seeking the divorce. If the husband divorces the wife without any good reason, it is considered an arbitrary divorce and the husband must pay compensation to the wife. Then the court assigns two arbitrators—one from the wife's family and the other from the husband's family—who mediate between the husband and wife and try to bring about a reconciliation. If this fails, the two arbitrators decide which party is the one without a good reason to seek divorce, and that person must pay the compensation to the other. This system is in accordance with what is called the Hanafi School of thought in Islam.

The case for a Christian divorce is different because we have many different sects—Latin, Catholic, Orthodox, and others. Each of these sects has its own court with judges who are the priests of that sect and who decide who the victim in each case is. Each court has its own laws to follow; some sanction divorce and others do not. For instance, the Greek Orthodox court allows divorce. The Catholic and Latin do not; they would only approve of a separation. Then, if a separated couple wants to remarry someone else, they have to change their sect altogether. I think the society has become more open now and is willing to accept an individual's change of religious sect to get remarried. Some seek an annulment, but this is a tough case to argue because the plaintiff has to prove to the priests that the marriage was originally wrong.

My work with Christian divorce has made me realize that Muslim women have more freedom and rights in divorce issues than their Christian counterparts. In Islam, divorce is permissible, but does not take place very often. If it does happen, people think that the husband dumped his wife. This is not true. Unjustified divorce, as I mentioned earlier, forces the husband to pay compensation to the wife. It is similar to a settlement that one gets from an insurance company if one is hurt in a car accident. The court decides on the amount of money the wife deserves by evaluating the physical and psychological harm that the husband caused her by deciding to divorce her without her knowledge or agreement. Even if the husband had good reasons for seeking a divorce she still gets the deferred dowry, which is the amount of money or property both agreed on when they got married.

It is permissible in Islam for the wife to seek a divorce. In these instances, the court studies the case and decides which of the two has caused physical and psychological harm to the other. If the court determines that the wife has caused harm she will not get all of her deferred dowry. If the husband has caused harm he has to pay the entire deferred dowry, plus the amount of compensation the wife deserves. Either way, Muslim women end up with more than the husband. Plus, the woman keeps all her jewelry and whatever she owns—property, bank accounts, etc.

We also have the "redemption," which exists in the Holy Quran and Islamic Law. This is the case when the wife redeems her husband if she does not want him. Currently, this arrangement is a subject of much argument in society and Parliament, because since this law's passing there have been seventy cases. Here is an example of how it works. Let's say the wife sees her husband drunk or with another woman. She can go to the judge with proof, and the judge will grant her a divorce and allow her to keep all of her dowry.

According to Islamic law, the dowry is paid just before the marriage takes place, or is deferred to be paid upon divorce or the death of the husband. If the judge decides that the wife has been wronged by the divorce, he will order that she gets her dowry, the custody of the children, plus alimony to cover their expenses. In Islam, custody of the children is always awarded to the mother, which is not the case in Christian courts. In a Christian divorce, the father can get custody of the children simply because the wife initiated the divorce. In Islam, even if the wife gives custody to the husband she can get the children back whenever she decides to.

As an Arab Muslim woman I do not wish that I had been born somewhere else. Why should I? Others may see Arab women as oppressed, but that is because they do not know what type of lives we live. We do not feel oppressed. For example, many may think that Muslim husbands beat their wives, but my husband never beats me—and I do not beat him. I do not think that women are beaten except on television; this does not happen often in our society.

I do not know anyone who has been beaten. I have seen a case where a Christian woman sought divorce because her husband slapped her just once. I know through my experiences as a lawyer and as an individual that women in Jordan do not tolerate being abused or beaten, even by their husbands.

*   *   *

My husband comes from a family line of Bedouins, who are characteristically brave, generous, perspicacious, virtuous, and giving. I remember my mother-in-law always said that her husband never beat her. Even in Bedouin society it was considered a character flaw if a man beat his wife. A man who respects himself does not beat a woman.

Polygamy was allowed in Islam under strict conditions in order for the society to solve certain social problems. A good example is that in times of war many men left widows and orphans behind. If a man is allowed to marry a widow with children he can offer them shelter and sustenance. When Islam was founded 1,400 years ago in Arabia, the habit was for men to have a huge number of wives. Islam limited this practice and made it conditional, so that a man can have a maximum of four wives as long as he can support them and love them equally.

But polygamy in our society today is very rare; the reaction to having more than one wife is always rejection, at least among educated people. Islamic law protects the wife in cases of polygamy, and she has the right to file for divorce if her husband intends to marry another woman. The law now forces the husband to inform his wife before he marries again. In all my life, I've only known of one person who married two women, but only after he divorced his first wife. Polygamy exists, but it is very limited.

*   *   *

As a Muslim woman I am happy with my social status. My husband really helps me in my work and appreciates what I do and what I have achieved in my career. He takes responsibility for the household when I am busy. I try my best to fulfill my duties towards my home and children, but he fills in when I can't. My husband is the one who encouraged me to become a lawyer and helped me a lot during my training. I notice the same thing among my female lawyer friends and their husbands.

There are female judges, but I do not know the exact number; perhaps 25 in all courts except the Supreme Court. The reason is not because they are not allowed to be judges in higher courts, but because we do not yet have female lawyers who are old enough to be this type of judge. To be a judge in the Supreme Court you must have a certain amount of experience, and current female lawyers do not yet have that. We only started to have female lawyers twenty-five years ago, because we did not have a law school in Jordan until then. I must have at least twenty years of experience before I can become a judge on the Supreme Court. The few female lawyers who have twenty years of experience also have prosperous private practices and do not want to give them up to be judges who make less money.

*   *   *

As a Muslim I am willing to die for my religion. But I am also willing to live for many things—mainly my children, who I have worked hard to raise properly. I worked very hard to be a lawyer and have been through a lot during twenty years of marriage. So now is the time for me to see the result of all that work. My eldest son studies accounting. My second daughter is about to register at the university to study math with the goal of getting a Master's and PhD. She achieved a very high grade on the Secondary Exam, so she could choose medicine or engineering, but she loves math and prefers to study that. My family is my life and they keep me living.

Of course I am not willing to choose to die; to die for no reason is against religion and I will end up in hell if I do it. We Muslims strive all our lives to please God by doing good deeds so we can enter paradise in the hereafter. So, if one commits suicide he or she will end up in hell. Who would want this?

I can't put myself in the place of some Palestinians who willingly kill themselves. We live a different life from theirs; I am not suffering like them. We live comfortably and we have a stable and open society with no oppression or major political problems. We make our own decisions and have choices when it comes to how we want to live, study, work, and travel. But still our life is very hard. We work hard to provide our children with a decent life. We have no oil and we are not a rich country.

But the case of Palestinians is totally different. They are a people who suffer from the worst practices. They are deprived, oppressed, and live in a big prison surrounded by a wall. They cannot breathe or move around freely in their own country. Young Palestinians were born in a big prison where Israelis govern them with iron and fire. They have no hopes or dreams or ambitions. They do not see themselves born to live long; the actions of the Israelis force them to die young.

So if a Palestinian chooses to end his life, it happens as result of his own painful experience. For Muslims, committing suicide is prohibited, but Palestinians do not see it as committing suicide; they see it as dying in defense of a cause—namely to rid the Palestinians of military occupation. Suicide here is simply a war tactic. They use their bodies as weapons, because they have no weapons to face the Israeli tanks and missiles. They have no weapons to defend themselves against the helicopters shooting at them from the sky. They have limited choices and live in a constant state of war. In war all choices are open, just like when the Americans launch missiles that land on top of civilians indiscriminately.

These reactions by Palestinians are self-defense, since every Israeli is a soldier according to Israeli law. All Israelis are either active soldiers or members of reserve units that join the army when needed. There are no civilians in Israel. They are an occupation army. The Palestinians existed in Palestine for more than 4,000 years, before Moses ever set foot on Sinai, but the Israelis came from all over the world fifty years ago to occupy Palestinian land.

They still bring more Jewish settlers and place them among the Palestinians just to provoke them. Therefore, every Israeli is part of the occupation. Would an American sit idle if Cubans came to America and occupied it because some Cubans once set foot in some parts of America 300 or 2,000 years ago?

Some Jews say that Palestine is the "Promised Land" given to them by God, similar to Mecca and Medina for Muslims, but this is nonsense. Where is the document that says Palestine should be handed to the Jews? Let us see the written word that says the land is theirs. Where is the so-called promise?

For Muslims, Jerusalem is very sacred. We believe in all religions including Christianity and Judaism and do not exclude any religions or prophets. We believe in all the prophets and messengers—Moses, Jesus, Jacob, Muhammad (PBUT), and many others. Both Christians and Muslims know that the Holy Land has sacred places for both religions, not just for Jews. *God is not a real estate agent; the land is for all the people.*

Even though I am not Palestinian and not married to a Palestinian, the topic makes me angry. Why? I care because I am a Muslim; I can't see Palestinians being killed and feel fine about it. I care because I know the Palestinians. I live among them; every house in Amman has a Palestinian. I grew up with Palestinian neighbors. We see how the Israelis attack them in their houses, mosques, and churches. They are forbidden to go to the mosque or church and pray. The Israelis are in fact fighting humanity, not the Palestinians. I may not be married to a

Palestinian, but my sister is. My children may not be Palestinians, but my sister's are. How can I not feel their pain and suffering as humans on a daily basis?

        *   *   *

After September 11th America said that we attacked them because we were jealous of what they have, their superiority in science, democracy, and other achievements. They think that the attacks happened because we hate them. America is a country that is only 250 years old, yet it is number one in the world. We are 1,500 years old and look at what we have achieved. They think that we sit around and think of ways to kill them because we hate them.

I do hate them—not the people, but the government. We love American people; several members of my family are married to Americans. The wife of my husband's cousin is American, a friend of my husband's is American, and we like them very much. But the American government we hate because it is killing Arabs. Look at what the American government is doing to the Iraqis despite what they claim they have come for. This is daily genocide! They think they are right, but they are not. They are doing to the Arabs exactly what was done to the Jews. So of course I hate the American government.

People here now hate the American government in the same way the Palestinians hate the Israeli government. I mean, we have the right to live, don't we? We have the right to sleep without the sounds of explosions. I feel sorry for the Palestinians because they have to endure the daily killings and shootings. Every house in the occupied territories now has a martyr. Here in Amman, we cannot stand the sound of fireworks, so imagine how the Palestinians might be feeling when they hear the sounds of real gunfire on a daily basis. They die on a daily basis and almost all of those who are killed are civilians and children.

        *   *   *

I believe America invaded Iraq for its oil, because it was difficult for them to get hold of it while Saddam was in power. Saddam may have been a criminal, but the Iraqis had stability and security when he was in power. Some Iraqis say that they wish Saddam was still in power. The situation was not ideal under his rule, but any real change needed to come from the inside by the Iraqi people themselves—not from another country across the Atlantic through the gun barrel. By invading and occupying Iraq, the American government reintroduced the concept of colonial occupation after it had disappeared in the early twentieth century.

I say oil is the reason for the invasion because the only thing that was not attacked after they entered Baghdad was the Ministry of Oil and the oil wells. Other than that, the American army allowed robberies to happen and did not protect any other places. This was seen on television—even on CNN. In the past we used to watch CNN all the time, but now we watch al Jazeera (the Arab TV news channel). Arab governments do not like al Jazeera, and some are even banning it. The new Iraqi government closed the offices of al Jazeera even though they were supposed to have freedom of the press after Saddam was gone! I think al Jazeera is a television station that, to a large extent, presents the truth. It speaks our language and shows us what only foreign stations are courageous enough to show. They are open to all people; they interview Arabs, Americans, and Jews.

I do not think that the Americans will withdraw from Iraq, at least not before they get what they came for. Unless they face fierce and continuous resistance, the Americans will not leave Iraq. I think they should leave; I say this as a lawyer because the U.S. staying in Iraq is simply illegal. Some people were afraid that after the U.S. created the mess in Iraq a civil war would break out, and that by staying they will prevent this from happening. Well, look at Lebanon after the civil war. It literally grew up. It is stable and moving in the right direction. So maybe the same thing will happen to Iraq; maybe they will not fight over power and maybe they will. But imposing American leadership on them will not work, even if Iyad Allawi is a good person and has good qualities.

As long as he is perceived by the Iraqis as America's man, he will be resisted and challenged. The longer the Americans stay, the more complicated things in Iraq will be.

*   *   *

As an Arab lawyer who likes the American people I would like to tell the American president that he needs to treat us the way he treats Americans. Anything that he accepts for the Americans should be accepted for us. We went through bad political circumstances in the past few decades, but now we are working hard to improve ourselves using America as a model. So, as we all condemned the criminal actions of September 11th and the death of innocent people, we ask Americans to condemn the killing of Iraqis and Palestinians. We are a nation that has the right to live the same way you have the right to live. We are as human as you are. Americans will force their president to be even-handed with the Arabs only when they start seeing us as equals and realize that we have many things in common with them.

I think that the biased policy of America towards Israel affects the Arab nations' point of view; this is the main issue, the basis of all the problems in the Arab world—more than Afghanistan and more than Iraq. The Iraqis are still able to free themselves. Despite their current bad situation now, the Iraqis have not reached the level of misery of the Palestinians. Iraq is a capable nation with tremendous wealth, a vast country.

But the situation in Palestine is totally different. As a Muslim, you are angered because religious places are being attacked and threatened. As an Arab and as a human being, you are angered because you see genocide taking place right in front of your eyes.

If America sanctions the killing of an elderly person coming out of a mosque after prayers as self-defense, but at the same time does not accept the bombing of a bus full of soldiers who kill civilians, then it seems as if the U.S. government wants a whole nation to be wiped out (Palestinians) and another one to live

(Israelis). When the American government treats us as a nation that has the right to live as much as the Israelis, then Arabs will no longer be angry with the American government.

As a people and a country we have no quarrel with America. Actually, I would love to live the way Americans live. I think that people in America have a more relaxed life style than we have here. If you work hard, you achieve results and can climb up the ladder and reach the highest ranks in a company or an institution. Here the situation is different; your promotion is determined by factors like personal relations, nepotism, family connections, and political background.

I visited the States only once in 1983 for a short period of time and I liked it. My husband studied in Dallas, Texas, so we visited that city and visited all his professors at the university. They all liked him and the professors invited us to their homes and liked me as an Arab woman. We really enjoyed ourselves. I was also invited to dinner by a few Americans I got to know when we worked together at the Income Tax Department.

It is so sad that, at this period in time, the image of America is changing so negatively. America has drastically changed its foreign policy and has become unconditionally biased against Arabs and towards Israel. I am afraid that soon people will start to not like the Americans themselves and I do not want to see this happen.

I still have relations with the U.S. For example, my children recently went to the website of the university where their father studied and got the address of his favorite professor. My husband was very happy, as he feared that the professor might have passed away.

If my son wanted to go to the U.S. to study I would not mind. The U.S. is still very advanced in science and technology. My son would like to become a CPA in order to improve himself. If he decides to go to the U.S., then I will support him.

The one thing I like most about being an Arab is the security. We have total security; if you go home late at night you have no fear at all. I live in the suburbs of Amman, so if I am

driving home alone, I will have no fear. For example, the other
night I was going home alone after ten pm. There was a police
patrol doing a traffic check, and when they saw that I was a woman
and alone they did not make me stop; they signaled for me to move
on. This is the security we have in Jordan.

*If I could ask questions of Americans, they would be, "Why do you
find it too much for us to live like others? Why do you want us to
live inferior to others? Why do you want us to die without
exercising our right to self-defense? Why is it too much for us to
enjoy the natural wealth and resources that God gave us?"*

Khaled in his traditional religious costume

Khaled, **43**
Preacher and Professor
Cairo, Egypt
Muslim

Those of us with moderate voices suffer from media oppression. The media quotes unqualified people and makes them seem as if they are an authority on Islam....We think [September 11th] was an inhuman, immoral, tragedy that should not have happened to any country, regardless of religion.

Introduction

I felt that, during the course of this book project, I needed to talk to a Muslim preacher—especially because several American clergymen had sent me questions to pose to Arabs. I had one such tentative interview arranged while in Kuwait, but the cleric was out of the country.

I tried again in Egypt and was given many names and phone numbers, but none of my efforts resulted in scheduled interviews. I even tried to interview women advocates or teachers, but failed to establish any contacts. A few days before I was to leave Cairo I called one last number that had been given to me. It was very late—after midnight—but the man answered.

I introduced myself and told him that I was an American Muslim writing a book of Arab answers to American questions. He did not ask me who I was working for or who my publisher was; he just agreed to an interview on the following Wednesday afternoon at an office of the University where he teaches.

The ride to this meeting took about thirty minutes and passed modern buildings, a desert, an oasis with palm trees, the three Pyramids, and a few scattered cattle—an amazing amalgam of contradictions in time, space, color, ancient history, modernity, and nature. Egypt is the only country I have visited that can provoke all this in one scene, one moment of time. You can drift from one era to another in an instant.

In Egypt I feel that I can be anything I want; all I need is to try. In the midst of these extraordinarily positive thoughts, I rode in the back seat of an Egyptian taxi on an unusually hot October day. Fasting for Ramadan, suffering terribly from a cold and lack of medication, and barraged by an overly talkative driver, I had blurred vision and a splitting headache by the time I met Khaled.

I had not seen a photo of Khaled, so I did not know what he would look like; I expected an older man with a huge beard. He turned out to be pleasantly plump and shorter than myself. He wore a smart grey suit and what seemed to be a week-old beard. He was very welcoming and enthusiastic about my project and said that he was willing to spend as much time with me as I needed. He was full of life, yet very calm when he spoke. He was so passionate and sincere when he started to ask questions of Americans that he almost made me cry.

If people like Khaled could get time on American TV, relations between Arabs and Americans would be much better. If only it were that simple.

Meet Khaled

My name is Khaled. I was born to a religious family in one of the most ancient neighborhoods of Cairo, al Sayida Zainab (Peace be Upon Her—named after the Prophet's daughter). My father was a government employee who worked in the Roads & Bridges Authority. I am the youngest of five children—four boys and one girl. We all attended the university and some of us pursued higher education.

I remember the loving relationship between my mom and dad. My father deeply respected my mother, who helped raise and educate us. My parents gave us a lot of advice, but also a lot of freedom to choose what we wanted to be when we grew up.

I chose to study theology as a result of my voracious reading. I started reading at a very young age and read more than all of my peers. This early introduction to books had a positive impact on me and made me realize the degree to which Islam impacted world civilization. I went to the Azhar University, an internationally-esteemed Islamic university, majored in Hadith (The record of the teachings and actions of Muhammad, PBUH) and graduated with a degree from the Department of Religious Studies.

I also obtained my Master's degree, thanks to God. My thesis was titled "Preserving the Soul in the Holy Quran and the Sunnah[5]." The soul is one of the most sacred things that God gave to humanity and we have a duty to preserve it. Almighty God has directed the universe—man, animals, plants, and the divine laws—to fulfill its desires in an organized way that does not contradict the interests of anything else. God the Almighty purified the soul and gave it good moral authority that made it the most honored of all God's creations. He asked his Angels to prostrate to Adam, the first human created with a soul, which shows how great and highly valued the soul is. I pursued my Master's degree with the intention of educating people on how great the soul is, and to show its high value in the Holy Quran and the Sunnah.

Islam honors the soul, personal freedom, free will, human life, and the inner and outer peace of a human being. Our behavior should not hurt or harm the soul—ours or anyone else's, and Islam has steps a person can follow to guard and preserve the soul. So I compiled all the evidence on this and earned my Master's degree with honors, thanks to God.

In a few months I will be discussing my PhD dissertation in the Science of Hadith by looking at one of the most comprehensive and important books of Hadith, *Riyadu al-Salihin* by Imam Yahia

---

[5] The Sunnah is a book of sayings and traditions of the Prophet Muhammad (PBUH), a second source of guidance after the Quran.

bin Sharif al Dinn al Nawawi. The book talks about manners, which I see as the foundation of religions such as Buddhism, Judaism, Christianity, and Islam. All of these religions call for good behavior and manners, and show people how to behave toward each other far more than they ask for people to worship God.

Good manners and good behavior lead us closer to God. The study of manners is a school of thought and almost a science on its own. Therefore, those in theology see that a religion with no manners is a religion with no value. It is just a lifeless manual or an attempt to promote a delusion that does not exist. In the Holy Hadith, the Prophet Mohammed (PBUH) says, "I was sent to fulfill the high manners." This was his mission and what he wanted for the people.

*   *   *

I am forty-three years old, happily married with two daughters. I live in al Muhandesin in Cairo, a good neighborhood—as they say here in Egypt, a neighborhood of the elite. I am an Imam, a preacher and a teacher at the Ministry of Awqaf (Religion). I also work as a teacher at Egypt University for Science and Technology and as an on-air TV host for religious programs at Orbit Satellite Channel. I have produced many books, cassettes, and CDs that deal with jurisprudence issues, verdicts, and the guidance of Islam.

People assume that because I am a preacher of religion I am old-fashioned and do nothing but read and teach! I actually have many hobbies; I used to play squash regularly, but not any more because I am very busy. When I was a student, I went to the Center of Fine Arts and earned a diploma in Fine Arts, graduating with honors in painting, calligraphy, and other types of fine art. Now I paint and play the piano, organ, and flute; I like music very much. I also like to travel, go to the movies, and listen to music.

My daughters study at a nuns' school and I have good relationships with the nuns. I visit the school and they invite me to give lectures on Islam. So you see, I have a good life and am not complicated or extremist in any way. I practice moderation, which is what Islam calls for. Did you know that the real test for a true believer is the ability to adapt to modern life?

The Muslim who can adapt to real life is the Muslim that God the Almighty wants. On the other hand, the Muslim who isolates himself from life and lives in seclusion is a Muslim who does not practice Islam correctly. This is clearly stated in verse 77, Chapter 28 when God says:

"But seek, with the wealth, Which Allah (God) bestowed on thee, The home of Hereafter, Nor forget they portion in this World, But do thou good as Allah (God) has been good to thee, And seek not Occasions for mischief in the land: For Allah (God) loves not those Who do mischief."

Now that I've quoted the Quran, let me mention some of its unique characteristics. There is something that only the Quran has called the *Isnad*—always knowing who the narrator is, what he narrated, why, where, when, and to whom. One of the scholars said, "Without the *Isnad*, anyone would have said anything whenever and to whomever he or she wanted."

I will give you an example. Let's say that there is a rumor that says the American army has withdrawn from Iraq. How can we be sure of that? How can we verify if this is true or not? We do not ask people sitting in cafes, restaurants, or clubs. We need the *Isnad* of this information, the true source. In this case, we would look to the Pentagon, the only agency that can confirm or deny this information. We do not go to the U.S. Commerce Department to verify this truth, because if we did we would get distorted information. The Pentagon spokesperson is the only authority who can verify this particular information.

The divine system is similar in Islam. God talked to one of the authorized spokespersons (Prophet Muhammad, PBUH), gave him the message (Quran), and told him what to say and how to say it (Sunna). In this way we know who said every verse in the Quran—where, when, how, why, and to whom. We trust that the words of God are truly His, especially when you read the Quran in

Arabic. The wondrous and divine nature of the Quran can only be experienced by those who are really knowledgeable in the Arabic language because of Arabic's strict grammar, punctuation, and recitation rules. For example, pausing in the wrong place when reciting the Quran can significantly change the meaning. Could a human write this well?

Another unique feature of the Quran is the fact that there are no synonyms in it; each word has a different meaning. The Quran also talked about scientific discoveries proved true 1,400 years after their revelation. These verses, revealed to an illiterate Prophet Muhammad (PBUH) through the angel Jibril (Gabriel), speak of DNA and the darkness found in the deep oceans—topics that could not be known by an illiterate merchant living in the desert.

If you want science, it is in the Quran. If you want history, it is there. If you want literature, linguistics, psychology, biology, mathematics, astronomy, geology, economics, rules for a civil society, or politics—you will find it in the Quran. This is why there will never be a need to "update" the Quran to make it compatible with advances in science or modernity. There are still many scientific facts in the Quran that mankind does not yet have the level of knowledge needed to discover. It is a book for all times.

Another way to confirm the authenticity of the Quran is what we call the *Tawator*, which means that all people quote from the people before them, who quoted from all people before them, and so on. An example would be to go anywhere in the U.S. and ask who the President is. Everyone would tell you it is George W. Bush. There is no need for me to go to the State Department to confirm this information, because everyone is in unanimous agreement. Similarly, there is full agreement from one generation to another and for fourteen centuries back that the Quran is the word of God and that Muhammad (PBUH) was a messenger. By the way, there is no other book in history that has this *Tawator*.

A third way to confirm the authenticity of the Quran is the phonetic *Tawator* of the book—the fact that the language of the

Quran is alive and still spoken today. It is not a dead language like that of the Pharaohs of Egypt, which no one speaks today. Linguists solved the mystery of the symbols left by the Pharaohs, but we do not know how those words were pronounced. We do not know the phonetics of the language because it died. The Quran's miracle is the fact that the language is still alive today without any changes over the last fourteen centuries. It is an eternal language that will stay with mankind until the end of time. The rules of the language—the grammar, punctuation, and pronunciation—are still the same, so the Quran has remained the same from the instant it was revealed to Prophet Muhammad (PBUH).

This is what we call the Science of Reading and Reciting the Quran, which has been practiced from the beginning of Islam without any changes, additions, or omissions. The best proof of this is the beginning of the Chapter of Expansion and the beginning of the Chapter of the Heifer. Both start with the same three Arabic letters *alif*, *lam*, and *meem* (a, l, and m). In the first, the letters are read as a word, *alam*, while in the second they are read as individual letters *alif*, *lam*, and *meem*. The same three letters are read in two different ways, which is solid proof that we read the Quran the same way as we hear it, but not as we read it or see it. This is unique evidence of the wondrous linguistic nature of the Quran.

*   *   *

I want people to know about a phenomenon happening on a large scale, not only with the Quran, but with other books as well. This phenomenon is counterfeit copies. And just like with counterfeit money there are people making false copies of the Quran and selling them as if they are originals. This is also happening with English copies of the Quran that change meanings to suit the authors' agendas.

People come to me with all sorts of English books that are titled "the Quran," but are written by unauthorized writers who do not even speak Arabic! Such books incorrectly translate many words. For example, the word "pagan" refers to the Arabs that Mohammed battled during his early years as the Prophet, but it has been erroneously translated to mean "Christians" and "Jews" in some English versions.

This is totally incorrect. In the Arabic language, Jews are *Yahoud* and Christians are *Nasara*; both are *Ahlu al Kitab*, which translates into "The People of the Book." These books are being sold in the U.S. with incorrect translations that ruin the relationship between monotheistic peoples. In the Arabic version of the Quran we have unanimous, worldwide agreement on the version of *Hafs*[6] narrated by Asem. In English, I like the translation of the meanings of the Quran by Yusuf Ali.

*   *   *

There is always much debate over whether religion should be taught in schools. I think the issue is: Do we believe that religion is important in life or not? If we think that it is important then we must teach religion in schools. Having a multi-religion society is positive. It means that we all believe in the existence of God and we all love Him. The difference is only in the ways we reach Him, love Him, and worship Him. This is the issue that we need to understand when we talk about teaching religion in schools.

Rather than stop teaching religion all together, why not teach it as the art of dialogue between different peoples? This is a subject that will help students accept the existence of differing viewpoints. Maintaining just one point of view will backfire on the whole nation.

---

[6] There are about ten recitations of the Quran, with the differences being minor variations in pronunciation. One of these recitations—used in Saudi Arabia, the Gulf States, Yemen, Sudan and Egypt—is the recitation of Hafs.

Children must be raised in a way that helps them accept others, understand the humanity of all people, and not see others as subhuman because their color or religion is different. If we can do that, then religion will be a subject that helps students practice love, sincerity, and compassion.

I would like to ask a question of people who do not want religion to be taught in schools: Do you really think schools decide which religion we belong to? Of course not. I told you my daughters study at a nun's school. Did that make them convert to Christianity or be less Muslim than their peers who go to government schools that do not have Christianity classes? Would a Muslim preacher put his daughters in a Catholic school if schools determined what religion to follow? My daughters are in a school that is run by nuns because I am confident that their religion will not be changed at the school. Christianity and Islam have in common good manners and morals emphasized in the behavior and discipline of the nuns. I want my daughters to be raised in a moral environment, so I chose this school for them.

Children grow up loyal to their parents' religion. Suppose that schools took out the subject of religion from the curriculum. Do you think that would mean my daughters would no longer believe in the importance of religion in their lives? No, because my wife and I maintain religion in our home and in our daily lives. A child will always belong to his home and parents. I really think that Egyptians will never agree with attempts to remove religion from school curricula, and I would call for the addition of dialogue among religions rather than isolating them.

I often meet people who do not believe in God. Perhaps they are secular because no religion could prove the existence of God. Would a Muslim or an Arab accept such people? I am going to be honest and frank, even if it upsets some: I cannot deal with a person who does not believe in the existence of God. The atheist has no control over the forces of life. Imagine that you go into a country that has no president or police force. Imagine a huge intersection without traffic lights or stop signs. What will happen?

You will fear for your life no matter how good your driving is, simply because you cannot guarantee how others will drive.

The role of a president is important in a country, just like the role of the policeman, parent, wife, and mother are important. Each one plays the role of a certain controlling force. The same goes for God, prophets, and holy books. They all offer ways to control forces in life. So, what is it that controls the forces for an atheist? How can I be safe with such a person? The Jews have a God; so do the Christians and the Muslims. Since these three have learned how to fear one God we know how to deal with and organize relations between us.

I know that it is possible for me to meet an atheist who has morals and treats me excellently, but I will not be very comfortable with this person or have a long-term relationship with him or her. However, this does not mean that I am allowed to abuse or harm this person in any way.

The Quran is very clear about this; a verse was revealed to Prophet Muhammad (PBUH) when a group of Muslims asked him how they should deal with those who did not accept Islam. Verse 60:8 (al Mumtahinah verse 8) goes like this:

"God does not forbid you to deal with those who did not fight you because of your religion and did not throw you out of your country to deal with them, to treat them with kindness and justice for God likes those who are just. But God has forbid you to deal with those who fought you and threw you outside the country and agreed with your enemies to harm you. Anyone who protects them is wrongful."

So, as the Quran says, if we have to deal with atheists, we must do so with kindness and respect.

*   *   *

I don't like hearing Americans say that the Quran says Muslims should hate and kill them. There are no verses in the Quran that encourage fighting with anybody, Muslim or non-Muslim. The Quran has verses that tell Muslims what to do if attacked—defend oneself against aggression—but it never sanctions starting wars or fights. Not one single verse in the Quran says that we must be aggressive toward others.

Islam asks us to die if we have to in defense of our land, religion, and honor. But as for attacking, this does not exist at all. I want people to understand that the verses of the Holy Quran that talk about killing and attacking are referring to being defensive, not offensive. Many people talk about events that happened 1,400 years ago and people in the West, especially after September 11th, misuse such verses and misquote them to try to defame Islam.

Many people also think that Islam forces others to convert. Verse 2:256 (al Baqarah verse 256) clearly addresses this by saying:

"Let there be no compulsion in religion, Truth stands out clear from Error, Whoever rejects Evil and believes in God Hath grasped the most trustworthy Hand-hold, that never breaks. And Allah (God) heareth and knoweth all things."

So any behavior or act of worship that is imposed by force or threat is refused and such conversion is not accepted. God states in the Quran that, had He wanted to create all people as Muslim, He would have. This would have been very easy for God to do, but He wanted every person to have a choice and use free will. How could Christianity and Judaism survive all these centuries in the Arab world if Muslims converted people by force? In fact, Islam preserved those religions and their holy sites from extinction. It was not Muslims who burnt Jews and Christians during the Crusades; it was not Muslims who burnt people in Spain during the Inquisition; it was not Muslims who forced Jews to live in gated ghettos; it was not Muslims who burnt Jews in the Holocaust.

Yet when you watch American media you find much talk about Muslim violence as if it is the only kind of violence happening anywhere on the planet. People keep saying that not enough Muslims condemned September 11th. I am a preacher of Islam, and I condemn it. Why haven't they put me on TV? Did they interview the Grand Mufti of Egypt or the head of al Azhar?

No, they did not. But guess who does get time on American TV? Osama bin Laden and his ilk. So it is no wonder that Americans think few Muslims condemned what happened. I always wonder who tells Americans that we did not condemn September 11th.

Those of us with moderate voices suffer from media oppression. The media quotes unqualified people and makes them seem as if they are authorities on Islam. One such example is a man called Abu Hafs al Masri. He appeared suddenly on the media scene in London and America as if he was the spokesperson for Islam and Muslims. Who is he? He does not have the education or the legitimacy to talk about anything, let alone religion. Yet he gets more time on air than any of us. This is a tragedy. To put a crazy extremist on TV is simply a tragedy for those who preach equality, fairness, and balance in media coverage.

*   *   *

Ladies and gentlemen of America, come to the land of Islam and find out for yourselves what Muslims think of September 11th. We think it was an inhuman, immoral, and unreligious tragedy that should not have happened to any country, regardless of religion. It had nothing to do with Islam.

Is it fair to condemn an entire religion for the actions of a few? Is it fair to blame Christianity for the gassing of the Jews? Is it fair to ask a Christian where the Bible says you should strip Jews naked and gas them?

I and many other Muslim scholars condemned and protested September 11th. I appeared on many Arabic satellite TV programs after September 11th and clearly said that what happened was tragic—the worst tragedy that has happened to Islam. Now people misunderstand the religion and Muslims everywhere will be oppressed for no reason. Even if the person who did it was Muslim (which I doubt) it is a disaster for Islam and does not serve it any way.

I doubt the existence of Osama bin Laden. I even doubt that he is alive; I think that he is a fictitious character like Don Quixote. I think bin Laden was created by the CIA to justify U.S. policies, wars, and occupation of foreign lands. I am a product of American movies and Hollywood, which taught us that if you do not have a symbol for evil just invent one. The American cowboy was given his native Indian to kill, the American policeman was given the Black to arrest, and so on.

I do not think that bin Laden called September 11th a holy battle. We live in an age of technology and imitating voices is one area where miracle-like advances have been achieved. Today you can make a film of someone with only one still picture or make people say things they never said. I have worked at one of the satellite channels for years and know how these things happen. So I do not trust technology at all. Even if Osama bin Laden exists, the great expertise and precision required to accomplish such an attack indicates that it couldn't have been done by amateur pilots.

This is a subject that even Americans have discussed. How could a few simple people hijack four airplanes and fly without interception by the most sophisticated air force on the face of earth and slam into important buildings? This action needed high tech equipment and trained experts to be able to hit those buildings with such precision.   Where was the FBI when all these so-called students were living freely and plotting this crime?

And who is this bin Laden who was seen on TV riding a horse with a rifle in his hand? This was like watching *Lawrence of Arabia*; it was sarcastic and funny and underestimated the viewers' intelligence. I do not believe in the legend of bin Laden. It is a legend made by Americans to fulfill a global plan to occupy the world. In all honesty, I almost admire Americans for their ingenious success.

           *   *   *

Of course there is Islamic fanaticism; there is no religion without its fanatics. Fanaticism is a human disease. A fanatic is someone who lacks logic, who cannot function in the mainstream and resorts to extremist means to fulfill his agenda. It is usually someone who is ignorant, cannot carry on a logical discussion, and does not know how to communicate with those who object to his or her extremist views. Such people prefer not to have a dialogue, because they will fail miserably.

Muslim extremism exists in degrees. I might be attacked because my daughters study at a Christian school. But that would not be "Muslim extremism." It would be the isolated actions of a small group of extreme Muslims. It is important to distinguish between the two. Islam is not extreme; on the contrary, it is a religion that stresses moderation, not only in practice, but also in worship. There are some ignorant Muslims who are extremists and do not have a clear understanding of how to channel their grievances or make sound judgments. If an ignorant person came to me swearing that the earth was square, what would I say to him? Do I swear back to him that it is round, or leave him to his ignorance? I would try to use logic and science to convince him that the earth is round.

However, the American administration creates many such extremists every day. When one feels he is being occupied, colonized, or invaded, you cannot expect him to behave like a normal person. When an Arab watches killings, beatings, and humiliations happening to fellow Arabs, how can you expect him not to react? And unfortunately, there is that small minority of extremists that react in a violent and ruthless way—a fact that only makes our situation worse.

We are a humiliated, wounded nation, a nation that has lost its resources, its right to speak, and its ability to express itself and resist invasions. It is a nation that, whenever it complains, Americans use the veto power in the Security Council. Whenever we ask for rights America threatens us with war. Whenever we ask for equality America makes fun of us and threatens us with sanctions. What do you expect of such a nation? Do you expect us to give you reformers and inventors who try to make the world a better place? I do not think so.

When you talk to Americans about their history of harming the Middle East they will admit fault, but say, "What about you? What do you do?"

They say we do not have democracy, only dictatorships governed by families and republics that are becoming royalty. But these regimes are protected by America; America defends them because they have interests there.

Some oil-producing countries are protected by America even though they do not have democracy. America can impose any democratic reform it wants, but refuses because its interests are best protected by repressive regimes. If there is any attempt to have true democracy in these countries, America will fight and destroy it because this reform will threaten the economic interest of America and its existence in the area.

I really hope that we do not brag about democracy because it is a big lie. Where is the democracy in killing and bombarding Palestine? Where is the democracy in attempting to confiscate the rights of a nation to elect their president? Arafat was trapped and isolated in his office, forbidden to move. America could have lifted that imprisonment and defended him if they wanted. But Arafat's movement and speeches and political activities conflicted with American interests, so they did nothing.

Ours is a crippled democracy, one that is dependent on and subject to American interests. A real democracy is one that respects others' wills and fosters equality among nations. The Israelis have the right to freely elect their president; the Palestinians should have the same right, but without being an occupied nation. This right is given to the Israelis, but not the Palestinians, and this is not fair at all.

        *   *   *

I feel that there is hope that circumstances will change in the Arab world and in America, but it depends on Americans. The American people are the only hope for change in the dark picture that Bush has created. The American nation is a great one; it is a nation that sets great examples and achieves the best in modern civilization.

But all that is destroyed by Bush—or at least he is trying to do that. If the American people choose a leader who represents what is great about America and Americans, then there is hope. If Americans tell their government not to build their economy and prosperity on top of the misery of poor and under-developed countries, then there is hope for change. Americans need to ask their leaders to give us a chance to express our grievances about Israel, a small country that illegally occupies another people—a country that was planted in the heart of the Arab world by Europeans to divide and rule the area. Creating a Zionist nation in the middle of a predominantly Muslim area represents a Zionist Christian ideology that is growing in America. This has to be changed if they are serious about reform. Our hope is built on the American people who can exert pressure on their administration not to interfere in others' affairs.

The American people cannot be hated because they are the people of a nation that has contributed immensely to modern civilization. Our problems do not lie with the American people, but with the Bush administration. We hope that most of the people in America do not agree with its foreign policies.

There should be opposition to lies and there should be actions. We want Americans to listen to Islam, but only through its true sources. We at the Azhar talk about Islam. Come and listen to us. Get in touch with us and visit us. Invite us to visit you and we will happily accept. We will show you the real Islam and how we see it. We still open our arms and hearts to you because we like you; no administration can separate us.

Religion is the force that controls the behavior of human beings. Two things have caused wars and mischief. First, the lack of knowledge of the true nature of religions, which call for peace, understanding, love, and the spread of good actions. Second, not following the rules and regulations put forward by religions. The defect really is in the follower, not the religions. There is no religion—be it Buddhism, Christianity, Judaism, Islam, or another—that calls for hatred and violence.

There are many questions I would like to ask American citizens:
Why do you hate us?
Why do you only hear from one side?
Why don't you listen to us?
Why don't you try to meet with us as we try to meet with you?
Why don't you allow us to explain our religion to you as you
explain your ideologies and religion to us?

Why are you so biased when it comes to Israel and forget that the
Palestinians are human beings who have the right
to live freely, just as you do?
Why do you expect us to welcome your armies when you are
destroying our mosques, schools, hospitals, and houses?
Why do Americans expect us to like their government when it
supports undemocratic systems?
Is it because you are not aware?
Is it because you care only about your interests no matter at what
cost they are fulfilled?

Do you really believe and trust that Bush is working for your
interests, or do you think that he is seeking personal gains by
finishing what his father failed to finish before him?

Do you really believe that the Bush administration has adequately
justified the war against Iraq, or do you realize that you were as
fooled as we were that there were weapons of mass destruction in
Iraq?

Where are those weapons now? How long will you wait for an
answer?

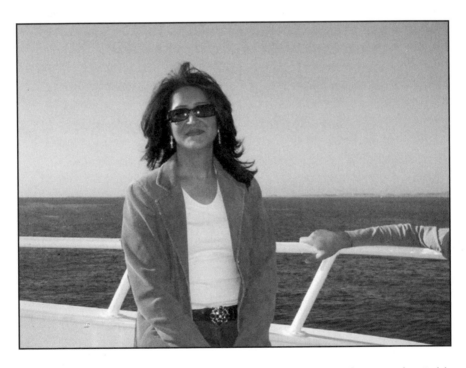

Haifa enjoying a sunny afternoon boat ride

Haifa, **43**
Engineer and Mother
Kuwait
Muslim

Everyone is a target of terrorism, even in the Arab world.
Just like many Americans I am afraid and I do not feel safe,
especially if extremist religious groups take over the
country… America can destroy terrorism simply by changing
its image in the world… In doing so the, U.S. will become a
credible force in the Arab world and can achieve what it
wants without the use of force.

Introduction

My trip to Kuwait was not initially on my itinerary. I never
intended to visit Kuwait again after my brief trip back in 1987 for a
wedding. I was born in Kuwait and lived there until my father's
death in 1975, when I was twelve years old. My childhood and
school days in Kuwait were a mix of extreme happiness and
extreme sadness. As non-Kuwaitis, we were treated like second-
class citizens by some, but we lived a good life otherwise.

My friend Hooda had persistently argued that I should
include Kuwait in my trip. She finally convinced me when she
said that interviewing Kuwaitis would give my book balance by
representing the views of Arabs in the Persian Gulf nations.

To my surprise, the trip to Kuwait became a healing
process. It started at the airport where all the young Kuwaiti
security personnel smiled and treated me with great politeness—a
rare thing when I had lived there. As I moved through customs, I
thought how amazing! Once I was a stateless Palestinian, and now

I was the citizen of a super-power that offered military protection to the very country that had mistreated me.

My heart raced as I took my visa and American passport to the customs window. The young passport agent looked at the place of birth and burst out laughing when he read that I was born in Kuwait! I did not know why he laughed and was not interested in finding out. But I think he was not ridiculing me; he was just surprised and amused.

I had many mixed emotions streaming in my mind and heart while traveling the empty streets that took us to Hooda's house. Memories of my father mixed with others of my childhood and friends, and I tried to remember the buildings and streets as they used to look. Suddenly I saw ruins—reminders of the Iraqi invasion fourteen years ago and was taken aback by feelings of loss and sorrow. As a Palestinian, I know what it means to lose a country, and was furious about Saddam and his disastrous adventure in Kuwait. At that moment, I felt that I was indeed a different person—a healed one.

But my healing process continued. My friend's husband, the owner of an engineering company, arranged the interview with Haifa. I was surprised to discover that he employed a number of female Kuwaiti engineers; Kuwait had changed after all.

I met Haifa at her tiny office in old downtown Kuwait. She was casually dressed and very excited about my project—she felt a need to talk personally to Americans. I truly never expected a Kuwaiti woman to be so courageous.

Meet Haifa

My name is Haifa. I was born in Kuwait and studied at Kuwaiti schools until I went to the university. My family can trace its roots to Iraq and is less conservative than typical Kuwaiti families. I think this affected my upbringing in a positive way.

My family believed in the importance of education—girls' education in particular. I grew up in a family of few males, so men did not play a dominant role in our daily lives. My immediate family consisted of our grandmother and mother, both of whom were widows. I have three sisters and no brothers. Men never had a dominant role in our household, which gave me self-confidence and a sense that women are equal to men.

During my childhood, my family spent most of the long, hot summers in Lebanon. We had many Lebanese friends, and their culture had a strong effect on me. Lebanese society is more open and free than Kuwait's, and I think my open mind is partially a result of this background.

We attended public schools that had students from Algeria, Palestine, Libya, Iraq, and many other nationalities. Our school supported the concept that all Arabs are equal and all religions deserve respect. Unfortunately, this is not true now. In Kuwait, only Kuwaitis are allowed to study in public schools these days; students of other nationalities have to go to private schools.

The quality of our education was truly excellent, but today's students do not receive the same quality education. Ours was better because when I was going to school the Arab world was focused on the idea of Arab nationalism. It was a movement that made us feel good about ourselves and gave us freedom. Textbooks did not reflect conservative trends or religious fanaticism.

Today's education has "craziness"—everything is centered around religion, as if people are guilty of something and need to purify themselves constantly. We did not study this way; quite the opposite. We studied the French Revolution and liberation movements, and this education was excellent.

*   *   *

I entered the University of Kuwait in 1979. I wanted to study architectural engineering, but that was not available so I studied civil engineering. At this point in my education I was ready for a new level of independent thinking, and what was available at the time was the socialist movement. I started to pay more attention to social and political issues, but was not interested

in becoming a socialist. Our goal as new college students was to
establish a free society without any social restraints. We knew that
restraints inherently exist in every individual; what we rejected
were societal restraints. We refused the ideas of sectarianism and
religious extremism that are not based on any ideology. It is
during this time that I became aware of the "Bedouinism" of my
society.

We students felt that Kuwaiti society was being dragged
into becoming a Bedouin (tribal, nomadic) society. It's not that
Bedouin society is bad; on the contrary, Bedouins have many
traditions that we respect and appreciate. But Bedouin women are
not treated with the respect or given the freedom they deserve, and
we wanted an open society where the freedom of the individual is
respected. Capitalism had a bad image, so we looked to socialism
to help us achieve the goal of personal freedom.

At the time, America gave the impression that it supported
dictators over democracies. The U.S. government supported the
Afghanis even though the Afghani Mujahideen (including Osama
bin Laden) were very dangerous and could not be trusted.
Therefore, America and capitalism were not appealing to us.

Those of us who lived in Kuwait knew how dangerous the
Afghanis were, because we dealt with similar extremists on a daily
basis; we saw them every day at the university. We knew their
mentality, political ambitions, and what they wanted. Even so,
they had support from all over Kuwait.

The support of such extremists made us realize that there
could not be any commonality between the openness that we
sought and America. We were also sure that the Afghani
Mujahideen (later the Taliban) would turn against the Americans,
but no one would listen to us at the time.

*   *   *

I do not believe in absolute freedom. Morality is an
integral part of my ideal freedom, which does not infringe on the
rights of others. I believe a person should be free to live the way

he or she wants and to express his or her ideas freely and honestly. I also believe that women are no less than men in terms of intelligence, abilities, and capabilities.

After graduation I worked for the Ministry of Public Works, which oversaw everything related to highway construction, and I helped build Kuwait's Central Highway. The company overseeing this project was American and headquartered in Washington, D.C. with a Kuwaiti branch. I remained with the company until the invasion in 1990, when they had to leave Kuwait. After the liberation of Kuwait, it was difficult for me to work; the whole system became different. I was used to the efficiency of the American system and was not able to continue in my job after the invasion.

I left the Ministry of Public Works and began working at the State Audit Bureau. It was not the right place for me, but the salary was good so I stayed for ten years. After ten years I decided to leave and joined F.J. engineering company. This job is perfect because I do business development and oversee some simple projects, plus I have a good working relationship with my colleagues. I have never been happier in my life.

I am married and have two daughters, ages fifteen and eleven. My husband is very supportive and does not mind me working—on the contrary, he encourages me. He usually leaves work earlier than I do and really enjoys looking after the girls while I am still at work. Here in Kuwait I wear what I want and work and go out by myself, but there are societal constraints I have to follow. By nature I hate any type of constraints; I am an extremist in this sense. I can't accept things that are forced on me. I like to choose who I want to be and what I want to do. For example, if you gave me the choice to walk naked I wouldn't do it, but I'd like to have that option. I like to do what I want to do as long as I am not offending anyone. I hate knowing there is something I can't do only because someone says I can't do it.

My husband never imposes things on me; neither does my family. But there are societal constraints. For example, women cannot go to the public beach to swim; we have to go to private beaches. If you swim at a public beach, you will get into trouble. You will attract attention. If I want to swim, I have to travel outside the country. People leave the country just to enjoy wearing a bathing suit! If you go to the beaches of Cyprus or Sharm El Sheikh (a popular tourist area by the Red Sea in Egypt) no one will notice you, because there are many people there. Here, no one goes to the beach, so if you go you will be insulted.

Sometimes my husband and I want to go dancing at a nightclub, but you cannot dance in public now. You could when I was growing up. Now we dance in private and at parties, because dancing publicly will get you in trouble. Kuwait has deteriorated because of the growing religious movement.

Do not get me wrong; I am not condemning Bedouin culture or Arab society. All I am saying is that there is something wrong with the way some men are raised. It starts in the home where mothers treat the sons better than the daughters. These boys grow up feeling superior to their sisters; they feel that they have the upper hand in the household, which sadly comes from the mother. The sisters have to get permission from their brothers just to go out.

Because of this men grow up with the idea that women are inferior. When they get married or start working they treat women as if they are fragile and should be controlled and kept in the background. This is a direct result of upbringing.

On the other hand there is something very great about our culture—the family ties. It is an extremely positive thing that American society lacks. For example, if my sister is a single parent she will get support from me and from the rest of the family. We would never let her face life alone or without financial and emotional support. But in American society a sixteen or seventeen-year-old girl with children might live alone and without family support. Being this young, she cannot raise a healthy family on her own. In our society, the whole family will look after her, which helps not only her, but society as a whole.

There is a major difference between the structure of the American family and the Arab family. Ours is based on family ties and sacrifice; the American is based on individualism and what I call over-self-centrism. In America, a person can simply stop looking after his family.

I also like the artistic aspect of Arabic culture and feel it needs to be developed more. We have great music and musical instruments that produce a wide and unique variety of songs. We have several different traditional costumes, arts, and crafts that reflect regional differences. We have a history and a heritage that is distinctive and rich and could enrich the whole world by sharing it. Unfortunately, we cannot give all we could because we are not free to invent and to think—the dictatorship of our government prevents it. Imagine if we were a free society like America; with such a rich heritage we would produce something really gorgeous.

Sometimes I ask myself if I would have wanted to be born elsewhere. It's a very difficult question for me to answer, because each society has positive and negative aspects. When I see what I have achieved, I feel that this is where I want to be. But when I look at what I cannot accomplish in this society, I feel that I want to live in a Western society. In general, I am happy with where I am and who I am. But I want to see change in our country.

*   *   *

I strongly believe in separating religion and government; many problems result from joining them. I do not believe that our problems have to do with Islam or its teachings; the problems lie in mixing the backward social beliefs that existed before Islam itself. I see Islam in Kuwait going through a dangerous stage of extremism that will lead people to abandon religion altogether.

Many people misunderstand Islam. Muslims should emphasize Islam's tolerant style, which makes people eager to accept it. These days Islam is linked to terrorism because of what I call the "retarded" clergymen who are personally benefiting from religion and making fortunes from it.

Let me be specific here and talk about the Shiites. I am a Shiite. I know that the clergymen are personally benefiting from preaching religion. This is a serious issue, and I know that I am treading dangerous waters by saying this, but I will say it anyway: The Shiite clergymen in Kuwait are benefiting financially from their religious preaching. They collect money for causes, but most of that money goes into their own pockets.

This is one side of it. The other side has to do with these same clergymen politicizing the religion. They are changing the pure nature of Islam into a political one. Where is the pure Islam? It is not there any more. They have linked it to politics and mixed it all together.

Our problems are not only related to clergymen and their outdated ideas. We also have problems when it comes to Arab politicians. They are as bad as—if not worse than—the clergymen. They lie and compromise a lot. If their political interests conflict with the public interest, they choose their personal political interests. They bargain and compromise at the expense of their constituents. Now imagine if religion gets in this political game, too. This will be a big mistake, because there is no bargaining or compromise in religion.

Religion should be about reaching inner peace with oneself; this is its ultimate goal. It is not about being a target for the entire world, but because you are targeted you fight back. Muslims think that there is an international plan to destroy the religion of Islam. Osama bin Laden believes that the world is plotting to destroy Islam; but this only exists in the imagination of people who I think are crazy. If anybody is really harming Islam, it is the extremists whose voices are being heard all over the world. Nobody hears the voices of those of us who truly love Islam, especially the West.

But how could they hear our voices if we are not even heard in our own societies? There are a great number of tolerant, open-minded Kuwaitis who are now suffering and are in constant struggle with the rest of the society. Sometimes such people just quit fighting for change because they get tired of fighting; they give up.

I will never give up completely. I will continue to write to local newspapers and take part in political activities and attend conferences. I think that the greatest role I can play is really at home with my daughters. I am bringing up my daughters so that they are strong—able to face resistance and help their society.

But for now our voice is not heard in our country, because the government does not give us the chance. Women do not have the right to vote in Kuwait, which bothers me tremendously. The Quran does not say that women should not vote. Men and women are treated equally in Islam, and even the Prophet used to consult his wife Khadija in political matters. How then can they prevent us from voting in elections and get away with it?

You know why we do not vote? It is because of the religious control exercised over the Kuwaiti Parliament. If Kuwait had continued with the nationalism of the 1970s, things would be very different—probably much better than what we have now.

*   *   *

Although I respect Americans, I think they have some responsibility for the growth of religious political power in our society. We do not want to blame the Americans for all our problems, but they have to admit that they have supported political Islam in the past. American support came as a result of the long war against socialism. They thought that extreme religious trends were the best way to conquer and defeat socialism. I totally disagree with that.

If I was in charge, I would want the U.S. to put pressure on Arab countries to allow liberal voices and trends adequate space to exist and be heard in the same way they put pressure on Arab countries to allow the religious extremists to grow and flourish. I would allow educated Arabs a major role in democratizing the Arab world. The extremist religious groups must shrink in size and influence, but for this to happen governments have to introduce realistic alternatives. The tolerant religious groups and voices should be strengthened. We are not asking for an atheist or a non-Islamic society. On the contrary, liberal and tolerant people believe that religion is a good thing.

The alternative to extremism should be a mix of what is tolerant in religion and what is needed by a modern, free society in the twenty-first century. For example, all school curricula in Kuwait should be changed. Most subjects refer to religion even when the subject is scientific or deals with non-religious issues. Yes, religion is an integral part of one's life, but we do not need religion when we are reading poetry or learning science or math. The curriculum of today's schools teach as if one is born guilty and should work hard to try to compensate for this guilt, especially if you are a woman. Simply being a woman makes you guilty. You must cover yourself, not talk to strangers, no one should see you, and you can't express your opinion. All of this teaches girls that they are guilty of something.

An alternative to this is needed; this is not the real Islam. Women have a role in Islam. The men who created school curricula should read the history of Islam and learn about the freedom of thought and movement of Muslim women since the days of the Prophet. The Prophet did not ever talk or act in a way that put women under attack. What we see now is a result of being backward and uneducated, and the mixing of the Bedouin traditions and customs and belief systems with today's world. The modern urban man who lives in the city and knows the role of individuals is different from the Bedouin who still wants to live in a tent-like world.

This is not to underestimate Bedouin society. But such a society was based on the search for food—a tribal society where if a tribe did not find anything to eat, they would fight another to get food. Women had a very minimal role in this antiquated Bedouin society. In an urban society, a woman has a major role that cannot be denied. It is not the best of roles, but at least a woman can go out and people can see her. What we have now is a group of men who want to lock women inside the house. What they want is a total disappearance of women from public life. This is an attitude that really causes anger among many in Kuwait.

*   *   *

The U.S. talks about bringing democracy to the Arab world, but how are they going to do this without solving the Palestinian issue? I think that America after September 11th is paying a high price for supporting religious groups, for not pushing for real democratization in the Arab world, and for not solving the Palestinian problem. The U.S. will keep paying a heavy price if its people do not start to realize that the Jewish vote has an influence on electing their leaders, and therefore American leaders cater to the Jews and support Israel unequivocally.

If the U.S. is genuine in its intentions it will have to find a solution for the problem of the Palestinians who are really suffering. They are a people whose land has been taken away from them by force; they are a homeless people. Every day that passes without solving this problem creates nothing but hatred, extremism, and killing.

If the U.S. does not want to lose its credibility, then it has to use its power to find a solution to this problem. The U.S. must deal justly with the Palestinians and must apply pressure on Israel to really solve this problem. There will never be peace without a solution to this problem.

The U.S. position on Palestine is a short-sighted one. They are dealing with this issue the way they dealt with Afghanistan; short-term policies and solutions that lead to disastrous results. This makes the people in the region have a negative image of the U.S. If America wants to be safe and credible it has to change.

This is very similar to what happened in the Soviet Union. On the surface, it appeared that the USSR believed in social justice and freedom and wanted to find a solution for the Palestinian problem. But the reality of the situation was different; they said one thing and did the opposite. The young in the Arab world see America doing the same thing—talking about increasing freedom and democracy, but doing the opposite. If America practiced what it preached it would have the support of all the young Arabs, because they would see that it was a country of justice, freedom, and liberty. If America wants to rid us of injustice, it should rid the Palestinians of injustice as well. This would give America stability and solve many of its problems.

There were a lot of factors that led to September 11th, but I cannot justify it; everything has a cause, but it does not justify the action or make it right. For example, a serial killer has reasons for killing—his upbringing, society, etc.—but that does not justify his crimes. To kill innocent people is never justified.

There are reasons why September 11th happened. Americans need to look into those reasons and ask themselves, "Why did that happen to us?" Discussing September 11th is not meant to reward terrorists for their actions or show them that their horrible actions led us to try to solve the problems of the Middle East. But, at the same time, we do not want such a terrorist act to be repeated. Therefore, it is important to look at the reasons behind September 11th. We all need to talk about it because we do not want the Arab world to collapse into chaos or become a time bomb that will explode. The Arab world is vast in terms of area and if it explodes it will harm the whole world.

Everyone is a target of terrorism, even those of us in the Arab world. Just like many Americans I am afraid and I do not feel safe, especially if extremist religious groups take over the country. Everyone has a role in fighting terrorism.

America can destroy terrorism simply by changing its image in the world. Why America and not another country? Because America is the one that wants to be the major super power in the world. If you want to play this role then you must pay the consequences. You cannot be a strong country without credibility. You cannot use power against all people and just kill many people in reaction to September 11th. America has to change its image whether it likes it or not; whether they support the Palestinians or not they have to solve this problem. In doing so the U.S. will become a credible force in the Arab world and can achieve what it wants without the use of force. America can impress the young Arab generation, and twenty years from now the whole world will live in peace—there will be no need for young Arabs to be angry at

America if she is just and credible. But if America stays unjustly biased in favor of Israel, she is threatening her own existence.

*   *   *

The way the war in Iraq is going is not helping America's image. I supported the overthrow of Saddam Hussein; it was a good step and could not have been done any other way. If we waited for him to die his sons would have risen to power and it could have been much worse. Even so, the Americans could have fought this war in a different way—with much better planning. There was a misunderstanding of the nature of Iraqi society and consequently a great miscalculation.

Unfortunately, the situation in Iraq now is distorting America's image in the Arab world more than the war in Afghanistan did. The situation in Iraq now is the closest thing to being in hell. America's rush to war without good planning and an understanding of Iraqi society is leading to an Iraqi explosion that will threaten everyone.

In the coming months or years, I can only hope the situation in Iraq will come to an end. I cannot imagine what will happen in Iraq if the situation gets worse. I suppose the country will explode in civil war. And if that happens, I do not know if Kuwait can continue to exist as a country; we will suffer economically. The situation in Iraq is connected to Kuwait, so we will have a very dangerous situation here. America definitely does not want that.

I think America should not withdraw from Iraq; they cannot leave us with an unsettled neighbor. Those thousands of young American soldiers did not go to war to leave Iraq unsettled. We are all paying a heavy price for this war and America must find a way to end it and create a peaceful Iraq.

I am not talking about the withdrawal of troops. What I am saying is that they should find a way for this country to be settled in one way or another. If the presence of troops inside the cities is not accepted by the Iraqi people, then they should not be seen. In

Kuwait there are American troops, but we do not see them; we only see civilians. So maybe the U.S. needs to do in Iraq what they did here in Kuwait.

America should be the last country to give up on Iraq. Since they are the ones who started the war, they are the ones who must finish the job. Abandoning Iraq is unacceptable and might cause people to say that having Saddam in power was better and less chaotic. It would be terrible if people thought that, because Saddam was a disaster. This threatens us, our children, our future, our country, our hopes, and all aspects of life. America should know this and act accordingly.

Determining what I would ask Americans if I had the chance is such a difficult question. I would like to ask them if they really think the situation in Palestine is justified and that the U.S. is acting justly. That is what I would most like to know.

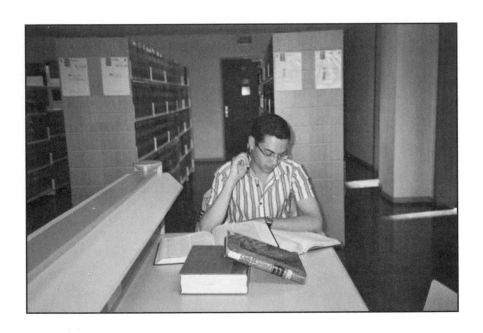

Mohamed studying

Mohamed, 19
Student
Cairo, Egypt
Muslim

It is time for the American people to pay attention to real news, to stop reading the same corporate newspapers and watching the same profit-driven media that has been misleading them all this time. Maybe then they will learn something about what is really going on in the world. Americans read their papers and watch their TV and think that every word said is true. It is a shame that such a rich country can have citizens who are so ignorant about world affairs.

Introduction

The young Arabs I see today in the Arab world are not like those I saw when I lived there fifteen years ago. Most of today's Arab teenagers dress, talk, and look like their American counterparts and even use American slang words like "cool" and "dude." Young Arabs and Americans have been brought closer together through the Internet, and this was clearly evident in the three countries I visited. The oversized sloppy pants, gelled hair, and layers of t-shirts are becoming the dress code of the young in the Arab world.

I often wonder if these teenagers have an opinion about their countries, political systems, the U.S., and wars. I managed to talk with a few, and those I spoke with were obsessed with chatting on the Internet! Many had friends all over the world that they had never met. Could the Internet bring these teenagers closer together? Is this going to be the generation that is less prone to war and more interested in communication?

My seventeen-year-old nephew Hashem just started college, where he is studying economics. He has very interesting friends who buy more hair gel in one month than most hair salons buy in a year. In fact, my hair gel and hairspray disappeared from my room the second day of my stay at my sister's house.

My nephew and his friends do not normally talk about politics, but they were eager to do so with me. It was not so much that I inspired them to have political discussions, but rather, with my years in America, I was "speaking their language," even though I was much older than they were. I felt that my nephew's friend Mohamed was unique; he is not your average teenager. While he did not leave me feeling optimistic about the present, in many ways, he left me with great hope for the future.

Meet Mohamed

My name is Mohamed. I was born in Cairo in 1986. I have one younger brother who loves music, especially American and European pop singers. I spent three or four years of my childhood in Germany—my dad worked there in agricultural technology. As soon as my family returned to Egypt I entered a French Jesuit school, which was my first eye-opening experience.

After that I went to an English school, which was very different from the French. I liked the students in the new school more than the teachers, who were very aloof. Many teachers emphasized that "Britain is the gateway to Europe," which made me feel like they thought they were still living in the old empire.

We used to debate our British teachers about the IRA— whether they were terrorists or freedom fighters. When the Iraq war started, the teachers told us about the English soldiers and their aptitude—how they could fight better than the American soldiers. In my opinion, even if you're better at a sin you're still sinning, so what difference does it make if you are better?

Later I moved to France to be with my sick grandmother. Living in several different countries had a profound impact on my way of thinking. I had some preconceptions about American and English people that were quite superficial. Slowly I started to believe that people in general are not that bad and one must be ready to listen to what other people have to say before making up one's mind about them.

I have very interesting parents who are complete opposites. My dad is a "Nasserite"—someone who believes in the political and social ideas of Gamal Abdel Nasser, Egypt's second ruler after the end of the monarchy in 1952. My mom is completely the opposite; she believes in capitalism and feels that Egypt should be more open in all aspects of life.

I prefer to think in a more global way—not institutionally or in terms of international organizations, but on an individual level. I think that if people would put less emphasis on religion and politics they would open up, understand each other better, and cooperate.

> *   *   *

I am not against religion; however, I feel it should be practiced on an individual level. Once religion is used on a mass level it becomes propaganda, a brainwashing tool. This has been true with all religions of the world. But when you practice religion on an individual level, it becomes a means to freedom, to believing in what you want to believe in.

I do not like any sort of propaganda and brainwashing, especially if done by government institutions. I will give you a funny example. I met a French university professor who told me that he steered a nuclear submarine for a few minutes while touring the U.S. as a guest of the American government. The program invited educators and members of the media from all over the world to make people pro-America. This professor got whatever he asked for—he even got to see Mexicans crossing the border in California. But even after all the American government did for him, he still left feeling anti-American. The U.S. government can spend a lot of money trying to make people pro-American, but end up achieving the opposite result.

I had a very interesting experience recently. My aunt asked me if I could help with a project she was doing for her university. I had to think for two or three weeks before I decided to do it; I did not know much about the project when I agreed to it, but became very interested when I saw the details. My job was to translate the meaning of the Quran into French for teenage readers. I have to point out that I was not doing a literal translation of the Quran; no one can do that. I was paraphrasing and translating, and this was not an easy task for me because I am not a strong believer in religion. It took me about three months to finish the project.

It worked out very well, because I had never intended to read the Quran. When I did, however, I found it to be very interesting. It didn't change my opinion about religion, but it greatly enriched my knowledge of religious thinking and methodology.

We studied religion in school, but it was not an efficient system—we just memorized a few verses and had lessons about how to treat people, but that was all. I could not talk to my friends about the issues and interesting points I discovered while working on the project or share this enriching experience with them because they do not know much about religion.

My parents never pushed religion on me, although my father is religious and his faith is very important to him. He believes that his faith explains everything in life, but he never tried to make me go to the mosque or practice religion. He told me once that I was smart and that, because religion was very self-explanatory, one day I would eventually be convinced. I argue with him over religious issues, and he tells me that religion is logical enough and strong enough to hold its footing against my arguments.

I do not doubt the importance of religion. I just feel that regarding religion—any religion—as an institution is not going to work well for anyone. If you regard it as a means to a continuous process of living, then religion becomes much more enriching.

I read a lot about other religions. They are all very interesting and point to the same goal, but you can get to this goal through other ways of thinking—other "perfectionist" thinking. Besides, nothing is perfect, and any religion can be twisted and used to justify horrible things. I will give you an example with Islam and violence.

There is a verse in the Quran that says something to the effect of, "If you kill any human for any reason other than self-defense, it is as if you have killed all of humanity." The meaning is so clear, but a person can still find a reason to kill by twisting other passages from the Quran; it's not that hard.

*　　　　　*　　　　　*

I'm going to France again in a couple of weeks, this time to study international law. I prefer philosophy, but my parents wanted me to study something I could pursue as a career. I like law and international law; I have done some reading on both and find it to be very interesting. Law is about claiming your rights and freedom, about being free to think for yourself. It is what led to the French Revolution, for example. If you are not given this freedom to think, then play by the rules and follow international law and you can achieve what you want.

*　　　　　*　　　　　*

I consider myself an Egyptian. What I like most about being an Egyptian is the country itself; it's just so beautiful and has so much history and culture. It is the simple things in life that make me happy—warm and welcoming people, for example. I don't feel that I am very Arab, especially when I meet people from other Arab countries. I think we are very different, but we have a gift that connects us—the Arabic language. Some Arabs—Algerians, for example—have a very strong accent, so I have to speak in French with them because I don't understand a word of what they say in Arabic!

I get along very well with French people. They have this non-neutral way of thinking, and being neutral in my opinion is the worst thing that can happen to a people's way of thinking. The French always have strong opinions about things. I don't have to agree with them, but they offer something to talk about, to ponder.

I do not get along very well with Americans because they treat everything with superficial universality. I've met Americans through my dad who works with many, and there are a few American teachers in my school. They are all very nice people, but when you go out to dinner with them you do not talk about politics or have existential conversations.

Americans are different from the French I've met—they are less opinionated, but more critical about politics. A conversation with Americans usually leads to a statement that they do everything better than the rest of the world, and I do not think that one can be sure of this about any nation. The Americans and the French are very different in so many ways—for example, the issue of the *hijab* hair cover for women. The French government has a "black and white policy" about this; it feels that *hijab* and other religious symbols are not in accordance with the concept of separation of church and state, so they made a law banning *hijab*. They did not offer excuses; they stuck with their decision. They never said that the *hijab* looks ugly or told people that wearing such symbols was stupid. They just banned it. American newspapers, on the other hand, are full of cartoons making fun of women with hair covers, but they will not ban *hijab*! The *hijab* is ridiculed, but not banned.

*   *   *

I do not feel like I am living in a crisis, but as a country and a region I know that we are. We think that we are perfect and we never face the truth; the whole Arab region does not face the truth. We do not have long-term strategies and do not plan ahead. We need to change everything, and this will take a long time—probably fifty years. Change will come through evolution, not revolution. It will not happen through a coup d'état. We have to let the natural course of history take its path. Maybe when my generation is older we will cause change.

Our leaders came to power a long time ago and think they are invincible. They start to believe what they say, that they are doing the right thing. And then they end up being dictators. The system of moving from one dictatorial president to another will not last; people will change the constitution and seek open and free democratic elections. We need a constitution that says a president can remain in power five or seven years at most. I do not want change to happen through a coup or a revolution, because the people who get to the top will stay at the top and the revolution will turn into a dictatorship.

No country in the world started as a democracy. People here need to get to the point where they have enough experience with democracy to realize that democracy is good for everyone, even if you do not like the result of voting. Currently, there are no real elections in any Arab country. I believe that change and democracy in the Arab world will not come through the U.S., because I don't think the U.S. has real democracy. How can it give democracy to the Arabs if it doesn't even have true democracy itself?

I was outraged when I went to see the Michael Moore movie *Fahrenheit 9/11*, which showed that many black people in Florida weren't allowed to vote. What kind of democracy is that? Are we going backwards in history? Most people think slavery and racism in America ended years ago; I used to think it ended after Martin Luther King, Jr. was assassinated. But obviously it hasn't ended, and may never end. If you're black and don't have the right to vote in a presidential election, that is ridiculous.

Arabs will evolve and develop their own model of democracy. It will take time and has to be done through peaceful means. I do not agree with people using violence to achieve political ends. The bombing of the Taba Hilton in the summer of

2004 was a disgrace. Egypt has been through several wars and we have reached the conclusion that we could get back what is rightly ours through international law and mediation. This is how we got Taba (a small area in the Sinai Desert that was to be handed back to Egyptian sovereignty) when Israel refused to hand it back to Egypt, as stipulated in the Camp David Peace Accords.

It was wrong to bomb people who came to celebrate a holiday. The Israelis came to have fun in the Sinai and had no bad intentions. Bombing the hotel where they were staying was terrible. This attack violated our peace treaty with Israel and was wrong. We are the ones who did not keep the peace that time.

I know that Israel breaks treaties too, but Egypt is no angel. I have a feeling that the Palestinians did it because they were angry at what Israel is doing in the occupied territories. Palestinians come to Egypt for education and medical treatment and should have never done this in Taba. It is one thing to kill in self defense or to fight to gain national freedom, but to kill civilians is terrorism—at least in my book.

People often confuse certain forms of "terrorism," however, with what, under international law, is national resistance. What al Qaeda does is terrorism. I do not like to use the term "al Qaeda" because it has a very loose definition. The media label anyone who believes that political ends can be met through violence as a member of al Qaeda, and this is not accurate. There are many different groups that believe in this concept, but are not connected to al Qaeda or bin Laden. If we lump all violent groups together, then people get the false notion that the institution is large and has many members. And this is making al Qaeda seem like a larger institution than it is.

The actions of al Qaeda are very different from what is going on inside Palestine. In World War II, the French resisted the German occupation with every means available to them. The Egyptians resisted the British, the Algerians resisted the French, and the Americans resisted the British. What is going inside Palestine is a similar war; it is very unfortunate that it has continued for so long. But it is a war—not terrorism.

Under international law, Palestinians have the right to resist occupation. When Palestinians attack military checkpoints inside their own occupied territories or attack occupation soldiers in their territories they are claiming their national sovereignty. But when Palestinians attack civilians it is terrorism.

Every country in the world has the right to resist occupation except the Palestinians. Every country in the world has the right to live freely except the Palestinians. Why is this? Is it because Palestine is not a country? I have a coin from Palestine, minted before 1948, that says "Palestine" on it. How can people claim that there was no country called Palestine? The claim that this area belonged to the Jewish people many thousands of years ago is historically inaccurate. Jews were in Egypt first so why don't they claim Egypt? Why doesn't Egypt claim Palestine—Egypt had a long presence there, as did many other dynasties. Why is it only the Jews who should have an historic claim to Palestine?

What I think of Israel as a neighbor is different from what I think of Israel as a country. As a country I think Israel is based on religion. It is racist and fascist, but I can coexist with Israel as a neighboring country.

I still think that this mess can be solved. It will not happen if you teach the young to be neutral and non-opinionated. They have to be taught to respect peace. We have to help the young see that there is so much for everyone to gain from peaceful coexistence.

I hope I see this in my lifetime. I think it could happen if someone with enough political and strategic strength and personal charisma puts pressure on both sides to reach an agreement. Then it would be possible to have peace. The Israelis are not stupid; they want trade and commerce and are tired of war. They want to live without having to fight. Not even the Arabs want war.

But still you have to give the Palestinian people their basic rights. No power can solve this problem without giving the Palestinians their rights. I think this can be solved by international law. We never gave up on Taba, and we got it back by law. The Palestinians can do the same.

*   *   *

I thought September 11th was a disaster on a human level and a very important time in history on a political level. Its impact will be as strong as that of WWII. That war made America a major power and weakened England and France. I hope September 11th will make people realize that no one is invincible. You have to make peace with the rest of the world; you cannot just act like the big chief, as though no one is your equal.

Even if you're the only major power in the world, you're vulnerable to attacks on many levels. So, the best way to be safe is to be more just. But from what I see, America has not changed how it handles politics. The Americans I know from school understand this, but not the government.

I was against the Taliban regime even before September 11th. Afghanistan is very different from Iraq. In Afghanistan, the Americans had a bad motive for war, but did the right thing. They wanted to catch one man and couldn't, but they did free the Afghani people from the Taliban. Afghanistan used to be a modern country until the Soviet invasion; it had culture, museums, and theater. It was a great country.

Foreign intervention brought the Taliban, who offered nothing to the people and made it like the surface of the moon—totally empty! All there is now is guns and fighting. I hope the new Afghani elections go well for them.

Iraq is different from Afghanistan, and I was completely against the American invasion. Iraq had a government and a sound infrastructure. Many of Saddam's actions were illegal, but the republic was legal. His rise to power was a bad historical event. America could have assassinated him, but they ended up assassinating the country. The U.S. had no legal right to invade Iraq.

The U.S invaded mainly to revive their economy. The war was more about the declining power of the American dollar than about oil. When the dollar declines in value a war has always revived it. The American economy is based on the production of weapons; so wars become a source of economic revival. America is a strong country because it has a strong currency, so when the value of the currency goes down American power can go down, too.

If America invaded Iraq because Saddam was an illegal leader, then why did they not invade Libya too? Qadafi is an absolute maniac; yet Western dignitaries visit and do business with him regularly now. Just a couple of years ago, he was listed as a terrorist. His regime was even caught red-handed as recently as last year, plotting to assassinate Libyan dissidents and Saudi officials—yet he is still considered an ally of the United States, simply because he is now willing to maintain favorable economic ties with them.

The American public thinks it is because he surrendered his nuclear program. But all Qadafi ever did was surrender some old rusted equipment and claim to no longer have an interest in developing nuclear weapons. Well, when did he ever develop anything? I do not think he ever had a nuclear program in place. But he "surrendered" his country and now the West does business with him. He is still the same man; he did not change a bit. So much for international justice!

America cannot bring democracy to the Arab world by invading countries like Iraq, while doing business with dictators like Qadafi. Democracy will not come this way. The exact opposite will happen; there will be less democracy through such action.

It is time for the American people to pay attention to real news, to stop reading the same corporate newspapers and watching the same profit-driven media that's been misleading them all this time. Maybe then they will learn something about what is really going on in the world. Americans read their papers and watch their TV and think that every word said is true. It is a shame that such a rich country can have citizens who are so ignorant about world affairs.

My question for Americans is:
When will you stop believing all you read in
corporate-owned newspapers and watch on TV?

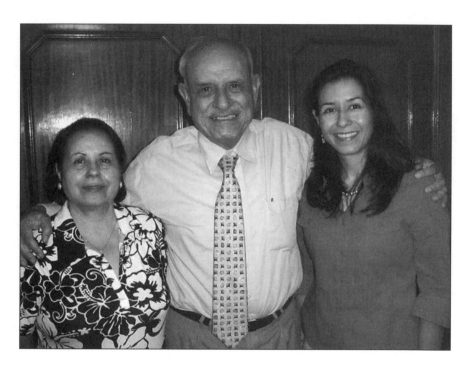

Dr. Khaled at home with his wife and daughter

Dr. Khaled, 68
Retired Diplomat and Professor
Amman, Jordan
Muslim

Oil is like air; it belongs to all of humanity. We need to deal with oil—like all of Earth's resources—in a mature and fair way. American oil policy is turning the blessing of oil into a curse and makes me wish there was no oil in our region.

Introduction

Dr. Khaled's name was suggested to me and I liked the idea of interviewing a retired diplomat. I felt he would be a good candidate to answer the tough political questions posed by Americans. I arrived mid-morning at his house and his wife and daughter welcomed me with a very tasty homemade petite pizza with *zatur* (Arabic thyme), tea, and coffee. Resistance was not an option!

Dr. Khaled reminded me of the government officials I interviewed for Jordanian television in the 1980s. It was a very fateful event in my life to work at a highly-sensitive government institution in Jordan, one that eventually led to my family and I obtaining citizenship thanks to a royal decree by the late King Hussein.

I had to remind Dr. Khaled that the questions posed were not my own, but that they belonged to Americans who did not know much about Arab people or the politics of the Arab world. He was very surprised at some of the questions and thought that I was no longer aware of Arabic traditions and culture.

163

This happened another time or two and on each occasion I had to remind the person I was interviewing that the questions were not my own.

I knew that some people might suspect that I worked for some American intelligence agency and would not believe that I was simply an individual trying to create a bridge of understanding and dialogue between Americans and Arabs. But I was openly suspected of this only once, in Jordan, and I felt both amused and upset by it.

I was amused because it was just silly. If I were working for an intelligence agency, I would at least be a bit discreet about my project. I felt upset because it reminded me that people everywhere have lost their innocence. A question asked of me many times in the United States and throughout the Arab world was, "Who is financing your book?" I am glad that I made the wise decision to do it on my own. It seems that this fact gave my project credibility and made people realize that mine was an individual attempt to bring two worlds closer together. Again, the world is no longer as innocent as it may have once been; everyone everywhere now more suspicious.

I never intended to interview the wife and daughter of Dr. Khaled, as well. However, both women really wanted to talk to Americans so, out of respect for their genuine desire, I have included the comments of Um Walid (wife) and Lina (daughter).

Meet Dr. Khaled

I am a Jordanian citizen now living in the city of Ajloun. Originally, I am from a village on the Jordan-Syrian border. I come from one of the largest families in the north of Jordan. My immediate family consists of my wife and our three children: Waleed, Alia, and Lina. Waleed is thirty-four and a First Secretary in the Foreign Service; Alia is thirty-three and a pharmacist; and Lina is twenty-nine, a dentist, and lieutenant in the Jordanian Military Medical Services.

I went to elementary and secondary school in Irbid, a small town in Jordan. In 1960 I began my political science studies at Cairo University in Egypt. As soon as I graduated I joined the diplomatic corps. I remained there for thirty-five years, retiring in 1995. I completed my PhD studies in Paris while working at the Jordanian Embassy.

After I retired I worked for seven years as a professor at several Jordanian universities. I now devote my time to political dialogue among intellectuals in Amman.

I am an elected member in three political organizations: the Jordanian Political Studies Association, the Jordanian International Affairs Association, and the Jordanian Writers' Union. My hobby is dealing with political issues. I would describe myself as a political intellect. I wrote a book on the Dead Sea and several articles that were published in a variety of newspapers. Recently, I devoted two and a half years of my life to write a book on terrorism.

I mention the fact that I come from one of the biggest Arab families because, when you talk about Arab countries, you need to understand the social and political structures of their societies. Tribalism is a traditional feature of Arab society, historically significant since before the time of the Prophet and Islam. A foreigner cannot understand the Arab world if he or she does not understand how tribalism affects the society and what it means. This sense of belonging to a tribe does not only exist in Arab countries; even Americans remember and mention where their ancestors came from. They say, "I am from Italy" or "I am from Germany." So when I talk about myself, I say that I am from the north of Jordan and from a certain tribe.

*   *   *

I have visited America several times: in 1962, 1978, and 1987. All of my visits were official and each lasted two or three months. I cannot claim that I got to know American society very well from these visits, but I read a lot about American society and politics.

I have a new way of describing America, which may be of interest to you and other Americans. America is no longer geographically restricted, such as to the States or an American Embassy. We now have the cultural Americanization of other places. So I say that America now exists all over the world. I can see America in Jordan through the way a Jordanian citizen walks down the street or how a Jordanian politician works. America is becoming an international phenomenon and America has a message for the rest of the world.

Originally, the American message was positive, but it has lost its way. I wish that I could deal with a pure America and not a Zionist America. I can tell you that there is no longer a pure America; all I see is an America under the influence of Zionism.

Look at how unjustly America deals with Arab and Muslim issues. The U.S. government sometimes does illogical things, things that are against international law when dealing with Arab and Muslim issues. It is confusing that such policies do not serve American interests in the region. I am not against American interests, but America has to serve its interests in this Arab region through the Arabs and not by taking sides. America must pay attention to all nations' interests and rights and not favor one country. I believe that if America changed its policies and was more impartial it would return to a pure America.

America is no longer an isolated nation; it has become a civilization. It gives humanity tremendous, enriching science and technology and still has so much to offer the world. But America loses its mind, logic, and direction when it is under the control of Zionism (unequivocal support for Israel).

*   *   *

Being someone who is as annoyed with terrorism as any American, I have a message for America: My country and others warned America about terrorism before most Americans even knew what the word meant. America did not understand the real meaning of terrorism until it hit home, in New York and Washington, DC. We were always against American support of Islamic radical movements, and what happened in New York is a result of American support for repressive Third World and Arab regimes. Jordan warned America of the dangers of terrorism; we were suffering from the consequences of terrorism before America had even heard of it.

America and the rest of the world need to define the meaning of the word "terrorism" if they really want to fight it. There have been many attempts to define terrorism going back to the League of Nations, which later became the United Nations (UN). The League was about to issue an agreement, but WWII broke out and then the world was busy with the war.

The world started to really worry about terrorism after the 1972 Olympics in Munich, where an attack on the Israeli athletes occurred. America wanted the definition of terrorism to be limited to its own interests and not have a total and complete definition of the term, because such a complete definition might restrict America's maneuvers in the world. Defining terrorism is like caging a wild animal, and no one wanted to do this. Everybody wanted the animal to be free so it can be hunted whenever it is needed. For this reason, I believe that there was a serious attempt to keep terrorism undefined. The U.S. kept the definition of terrorism an evolving one that can be modified to suit the description of whoever America's enemy is at the moment.

There are still many scholars and lawyers who try to define terrorism, but America always refuses. I know this because of the years I spent researching my book about terrorism. The term is now being misused; when oppressed nations try to claim their rights, the U.S. calls them terrorists. But alternately, when America tries to serve its interests by force it is not considered terrorism. According to America, violence is terrorism when practiced by the oppressed nations, but not when practiced by America.

Even though I'm Jordanian, I care about what happens in Morocco, Palestine, Malaysia, Indonesia—everywhere—because anything that happens around Jordan affects it. If there were no problems in Palestine then I personally would be better off economically and socially. I am obsessed with the Palestinian issue, which is a result of the American way of marketing and adopting it.

*   *   *

I think Osama bin Laden was trained by America, who later turned against him. The mistakes he committed are America's responsibility. But bin Laden does not represent Islam and is not a spokesperson for Muslims. Who would give that kind of a man such a position? It is very strange that people think of him as such, and equally strange that people think of America as the policeman of the world.

I sympathize with Americans for the despicable and disgusting act committed on September 11th, but I am not convinced that bin Laden or al Qaeda did it. I think this explanation was fabricated; maybe one day investigators will reveal how it all really happened. I do not think people are naïve enough to believe that bin Laden did it all by himself. As I told you, bin Laden was made by the U.S.

America has created many tyrants who later got out of control. The U.S. should not create such people. The fact that it does makes me think of the U.S. as a huge, inhumane giant that is blinded by power and makes a mess wherever it goes. I think it is past time for internal reform in America; I want America to be pure again, to go back to its ideals and values.

I know that the Arab world needs reform, too. Jordanians have worked hard to improve ourselves, to reform; we did not wait for America to ask us to do it. Yet we thank America. I am not sensitive about this, because I like America—just not America as it is now, under Zionist influence. For example, I prefer to deal with America rather than Britain, because America is a world leader.

It is important to point out that America defends "good," but does not fight evil. For this reason, I ask Americans to watch out for their government. I know that the American people do not have much say when it comes to their government's political and diplomatic actions. But they need to know that there are certain top government officials who put Israel's interests ahead of America's. They worked their way into the American political system and now advocate policies that do not benefit America. I hope Americans will show more interest in their government's foreign policy. When they do that, the ugly face of this policy will definitely change.

The American people need to begin paying attention to world politics and what their country does abroad. There is a real hatred for American international politics among Arab countries, a growing feeling Americans need to be aware of. King Abdullah II of Jordan has said several times that Third World countries are angry at U.S. foreign policy. Thank God this hatred is directed at the government and not at the American people, but I fear current U.S. foreign policy will change this. We have no quarrel with the American people, but we need them to reclaim their country. I say in my book, "O people of America, do not make American diplomacy a Zionist one!"

The majority of Americans believe that the September 11th attacks were based on an over-riding Arab hatred of American freedom, democracy, and wealth. This is ridiculous! We are fond of American democracy and admire American achievements. Arab parents are proud to say that their children graduated from an American university, because America has the best in science and technology. Go to American embassies in the Arab world and see how many people form lines, long before sunrise, to obtain American visas. This is a result of admiration, not envy.

Americans should appreciate our admiration, not refuse our love—and not ignore our causes. Do not deal with us as if we are vermin; wake up! Open your eyes and see the world with the ideals and values of a pure and compassionate America, not through a misguided, foggy lens.

I think that the invasion of Iraq was a mistake, a result of a policy put forward by the few elites I spoke of earlier. I do not think that America invaded Iraq for personal reasons; rather, it was a decision made by the biased.

       *   *   *

In the U.S. people say the Iraq invasion was motivated by oil; Bush, Cheney, and Rice were all involved in the oil industry. This mentality is not Zionist—it is more a school of thought that whoever controls oil will control the world. To a certain extent I feel this is true. Jordan has very little oil. We beg for oil; we need it more urgently than the U.S. In a worst-case scenario, the U.S can depend on its own oil reserves. But even if they did not have those reserves, would that be a good reason to invade Iraq or Kuwait?

Oil is noble merchandise and must be dealt with in a noble way. America is not dealing with it nobly; just needing more is not a legitimate excuse to try and take it all. If a country needs wheat, does this give it the right to invade and control Russian wheat fields? What is mine is mine and what is yours is yours. We can exchange and sell services and commodities, but not invade countries to take what we need by force.

Oil is like air; it belongs to all of humanity. We need to deal with oil—like all of Earth's resources—in a mature and fair way. American oil policy is turning the blessing of oil into a curse and makes me wish there was no oil in our region. If one of us envies the other, it is America who envies us—our oil, our strategic location. We did not go to America; America came to our region. We did not send tanks and soldiers to occupy America; America sent tanks and soldiers to occupy us.

Nobody prefers to see a theocracy (religion-based government) in Iraq. This is very clear. However, democracy is about people deciding for themselves what they want. So, let the Iraqis decide what they want. America will never be able, even with all its power and strength, to make Iraqis content with occupation. Iraqis are not dumb; how can they accept occupation?

Some in the current American administration say the Iraq War has improved the lives of Iraqis and rid them of Saddam. This one-sided attitude exemplifies what I said about America not seeing things with clear vision. America would be crazy to believe that occupation troops are liked anywhere in the world. Are there any foreign troops in the U.S.? How would Americans feel if there were foreign troops on their land?

I know that America will not withdraw its troops from Iraq—not unless they are forced to. Therefore, I side with the national resistance in Iraq. What is happening in Iraq is called national resistance; what else would you call it? If America would accept foreign troops coming to America and freeing them from Zionism, then Iraqis would be happy that America came to free them from Saddam.

*   *   *

I am not sure that governments based on Western-style democracy and civil liberties are a practical option for tribal-based Arab societies. Each nation has its own unique structure; no one configuration of democracy will fit the entire Arab world. In fact, the mistakes and the misery of the Arab world have much to do with foreign intervention. After WWI, the West did not give the newly-formed Arab nation states a chance to express themselves and show their true identity. Many European countries immediately occupied these new Arab countries. So the Arab nations merely went from Ottoman Turk dominance to Western control.

America has started to admit that it has wrongly supported the Arab regimes that are now turning against it. How am I going to respect American foreign policy when it supports dictatorial regimes? The U.S. does this for political reasons, for the best interests of a few people. We—the Arabs—have been occupied by the British, the French, and now America. Who is most hated?

America. Do you know why? Because the Americans in charge of foreign policy want to take everything and give nothing in return. Leave us to decide on our own what we want and make our own decision.

*   *   *

I am against mixing religion with politics and feel religion should be separated from the state. Islam is too noble to allow opportunists to use it for their own interests. Islam is a source of noble values; it should be left with all its great value and sacraments, not be dragged into the swamps of politics.

I do not judge countries by their predominant religion. Turkey, Malaysia, Indonesia, and others have their own special characteristics; Islam has nothing to do with it. In the same way, I do not think of European countries based on Christianity. We do not deal with America based on religion. Why do they judge us by our religion?

Many Americans think the September 11th attacks were religious-based, but that is not true. America created a business venture that went bad. When America talks to me it talks to an independent Jordanian citizen. When it talks to bin Laden it talks to somebody it made. So it is their responsibility. They made those extremists and now must take responsibility for that. I am not sure why America made these terrorists. Only the CIA knows.

*   *   *

Arabs always criticize the Saudi regime for being pro-America. Now America is attacking them because of the Wahabi influence in Saudi Arabia. So therefore, America has abused the Saudis twice: once for making the Saudis America's loyalists, and then for dumping them. In America they attribute everything the Saudis do to the Wahabis. But who encouraged and supported the Wahabis? America and the West.

The Wahabis may say they base their actions on Islam, but Islam supports the welfare of all humanity. There is no hatred or killing in Islam. It is similar to Christianity; both religions guide humanity on how to make the world good. There is no place in the Quran that promotes violence or killing. "He who kills not in self defense kills all of humanity."

It is also not true that Muslims believe all non-Muslims should convert to Islam. Islam has never forced anyone to embrace Islam. When Amir bin al Aas conquered Egypt he did not force the Christian Copts to embrace Islam. He protected their churches, which remain standing in Egypt till this day. Years later Egyptians began embracing Islam, maybe 200 years later.

In Jordan we have a theory that is proved true on a daily basis. We say that the creation of the state of Israel in the middle of the Arab world is what causes terrorism in the area. We never witnessed terrorism before the establishment of the state of Israel.

Israel is the country that started terrorism when its invading armies slaughtered the Palestinian inhabitants of the Dair Yassin village[7]. Isn't that terrorism? Isn't throwing one million people out of their country an act of terrorism? Isn't it terrorism to bomb schools in Egypt and Palestine? What do you call the bombing of the Ameriyya Shelter in Iraq? What do you call the atomic bomb in Hiroshima? This is all terrorism.

I believe that if there is peace in Palestine there will be room for Israel, for everyone. There are more than five million Palestinians living in the Palestinian Diaspora. If there is room for Jews in Palestine then there should be room for Palestinians, and of

---

[7] On the night of April 9, 1948, the Irgun Zvei Leumi surrounded the village of Deir Yasin, located on the outskirts of Jerusalem. After giving the sleeping residents a 15 minute warning to evacuate, Menachem Begin's Irgun attacked the village of 700 people, killing 254 mostly old men, women and children and wounding 300 others. Begin's guerrillas tossed many of the bodies in the village well, and paraded 150 captured women and children through the Jewish sectors of Jerusalem. Learn more at http://www.palestinehistory.com/mass01.htm.

course there is room. This is an issue that needs to be solved justly if the U.S. and others want to see peace in the region.

I cannot say what it will take for the Israelis and the Palestinians to compromise and reach peace. The Palestinians and Arabs are not the ones who created this conflict; ask those who created it when the problem will be solved. I created my own definition of those you need to ask. I call them the tribe of the "Balfours."[8]

Americans often think that Arab men see women as objects, not as equals or as partners. This is not true. I have always believed that the woman is a full partner and makes half the society. She has all the rights men have and also all the responsibilities. America's incorrect notion is caused by ignorance of the Arab world. Ignorance is the real issue.

My wife studied in Greece, just as I studied in Egypt. My son studied law and my daughters studied pharmacy and medicine. There is much misunderstanding in the West about the status of Arab women, all of which comes from ignorance. They do not know the difference between Saudi Arabia and Jordan.

As a diplomat and a university professor, I would like to ask a question to American diplomats and professors:
Can you be objective and fair toward the Arab world?
Can you be a pure American (one who does not always and unequivocally support Israel)?

---

[8] The Balfour Declaration was drafted by British secretary of state for foreign affairs, Arthur Balfour, in 1917. Through the declaration, Balfour established Britain's policy of permitting Jews to settle in the British colony of Palestine, without consulting the native Palestinian Arabs.

Dr. Khaled's daughter, Lina: I do not feel that the Western view of Arab women is accurate. Arab women have become government ministers and held other important positions. I myself worked with foreigners and have an MBA. People have to understand that not all men are the same. Some Arab men will not accept the idea that their wives have a higher degree or have a better salary, but this has nothing to do with religion. It is a cultural thing. Actually, Islam provides women with a lot of benefits; for example, no matter how high a wife's salary is, the husband is still responsible for her expenses.

I have no problems in my house or my relationship with my father or brother. But I know that there are some Jordanian men out there who do not like the idea of their wives making more money than them. Or they want the wife to take care of the expenses because she makes more money.

*   *   *

Dr. Khaled's wife, Um Walid: I feel that I lead a very normal life, have a strong personality, and raised my kids very well. They all have college degrees, and I have a Master's degree in home economics. I worked as a school principal and then as a supervisor at the Ministry of Education. As soon as I retired, my husband encouraged me to do charity work, and this is how I now spend most of my spare time.

A smart, capable wife can overcome the problems that arise in a marriage; some things are not worth quarreling over. Husbands can be influenced by their own upbringing, and this background can negatively affect their behavior. Some men travel or socialize with enlightened people, have good jobs and enjoy a good social life, and still treat their wives poorly—the way their mothers were treated when they were young. Other men change and become open-minded and feel that their wives are equal partners. This does not apply to all men, but many in Jordan and other Arab countries.

I ask you as an American woman living in this time of terrorism and war, what authority do you have over your husband or son if they decide to go to war?
How would you feel if they died in battle?
How do you feel when a Palestinian is killed by the Israeli army, or an Iraqi is killed? How can you as a woman influence all these events and the decisions made by governments?

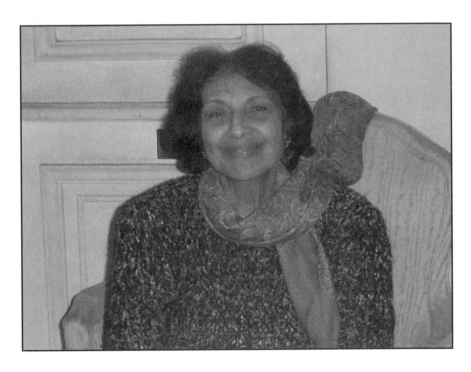

The dedicated Madam Soad

Madam Soad, 66
Angel to the Poor
Cairo, Egypt
Christian

I don't care very much for the U.S. government, I'm sorry to say. They are involved in too many things, too many wars. There is one solution to end fighting: if every person helps as many people as they can. Nobody that does bad things, like the U.S. government, and hardens his heart can be in heaven with the Lord.

Introduction

Madam Soad lived close to Cairo International Airport in Hilliopolis, or the New Cairo—a long drive from where my sister lives. The fasting month of Ramadan[9] had just started so I was fasting, and our appointment was early in the morning. I arrived exactly on time—a bit unusual when you are driving in a very crowded city like Cairo. Madam Soad lived across from one of the most ancient Coptic Churches in Egypt; she only had to cross a small street to get to her most beloved place in all of Cairo.

She waited for me on the balcony, and first thing she said was, "I cannot believe it. You are not a minute early or a minute late. What promptness!" It seemed that she liked me right away.

---

[9] Ramadan is the holy month of prescribed fasting for Muslims. It was during this month that the Quranic revelations began. During Ramadan, Muslims refrain from food, drink, and intimate intercourse from before the break of dawn until sunset.

Madam Soad used a cane and was barely able to walk. She was much darker than me and almost bent over. Her big house was filled with the French-style furniture Egyptians love. A huge Arabic Bible lay open on a table in her living room. She knew that I was Muslim and so assumed that I was fasting, but very politely offered me coffee in case I was not. Offering something to drink and eat to a visitor is a must in the Arab world no matter what religion or how rich or poor the host or hostess is.

I was very pleased when Madam Soad agreed to conduct the interview in English, since I would not need to translate it afterwards. As she started to talk about her beloved Jesus (peace be upon him), I remembered the dozens of times I had been asked if Arabs have ever heard of Jesus Christ. Now I sat next to a Christian woman who was totally consumed by religion and her love for "the Lord Jesus," an ancient descendent of the apostles. She shared with many Muslims the need for God in every aspect of daily life.

If Madam Soad entered a mall in America, people might assume, from her looks, that she was an Arab Muslim, but she can dispel several myths about Arabs. I hope that you will enjoy listening to her as much as I did and realize what a noble woman she is.

I must warn you that Madam Soad is a very savvy woman. I tried several times to ask her political questions, using every journalistic tactic, but to no avail. Nevertheless, she made several astute remarks about the political situation, in the context of her love of peace and Christian beliefs. She cares only about her religion and helping the poor. She is in this book because she represents a major part of the Arab world, the Christian part that many Americans do not know exists. Madam Soad shows that Christianity is alive and well in the heart of the Arab world; that serving Jesus is a daily blessing to a Christian who is surrounded by 1,000 mosques.

After leaving her house we drove through old Cairo on our way back to my sister's house. We passed many other Coptic churches and ancient mosques, saw the Salah El Din Citadel, and drove only yards away from thousands of graves, both Muslim and Christian. I saw minarets and crosses everywhere. I closed my eyes and tried to imagine who the dead were. Did they die in battles fighting the French invaders and Napoleon's army? Were they the dead Mamluks, slave soldiers used by Muslim Caliphs and the Ottoman Empire, who on more than one occasion seized power for themselves and were ultimately massacred in 1811 by Mohamed Ali, the founder of modern Egypt, outside the very citadel I now stood facing? There is so much history in Cairo, so much to learn, and so little time. The thought that came to my mind was simple yet seems hard to achieve: Why can't different people get along together the way different buildings and gravesites do?

Who knows, maybe Madam Soad has the answer.

Meet Madam Soad

I grew up in a Christian home, since both of my parents were raised Christian. I learned to pray as a child, and my family went to church every Sunday. I am sixty-six years old now and have been serving God for many, many years—maybe forty-five. Even though I've been serving him for a long time, my service and my love for the Lord grows ever deeper.

I graduated from the English Mission College, where I studied for twelve years, and then went to the American University in Cairo. Because of this I know English well, and I teach Sunday School in English.

On Saturday afternoons I teach two different age groups: ages five to nine and ten to thirteen. This year I made a new class for teenage girls. They have different problems, and in their own group they can open their hearts to me and I can better help them.

I thank the Lord for giving me so much love for him and for the poor. My two sons like their children to be with me sometimes, but most of my time now is for the poor. My sons are grown now, both married, so I am no longer responsible for them.

One is a dentist and has an eleven-month-old child, and one is an engineer and has two girls—one eleven years old and one fifteen. They all live in the same building where my husband and I live.

*   *   *

My active social work started twenty-five years ago when I went to Abu Dhabi in the Arab Emirates with my husband, who worked there as a pharmacist. I found people putting their old clothes in a basket and throwing it in the garbage or in the street. This never happens in Egypt, so of course I was astounded to see people throw clothes away.

I am a member of the Coptic Orthodox (Christian) Church, but there were no Coptic churches in the Emirates. There were many Protestant churches—probably because the English came to Abu Dhabi many years ago. So we prayed in an Anglican church.

In Abu Dhabi our pastor allowed me to make an announcement in church asking people to bring their old clothes to my home instead of throwing them away. My sons were not with us in Abu Dhabi, so we had an extra room that we used to store the clothes. I sorted them, put them in suitcases, and asked anyone going to Egypt to take a bag of clothes with him or her and give it to poor people in Egypt.

We stayed in Abu Dhabi for eight years, and I kept collecting old clothes and sending them to the poor and needy. I even asked the people in church not to throw away food, and to this day I meet people from my Abu Dhabi days who say, "Madam Soad, we never throw food away because you taught us not to." I used to tell them it is a sin to throw food away, because there are poor people who have nothing except a loaf of bread to eat, so thank the Lord for your food and do not throw it away. Many people are now taught this way; they give away old clothes instead of throwing them away. I liked my life in Abu Dhabi and practiced my religion the way I wanted without incident. I never felt that I needed to hide the fact that I was a Christian.

*   *   *

The Coptic Orthodox Christian Church was the first church in Egypt; it was founded by the apostles. Even our Pope of Alexandria is a descendent of the apostles. St. Mark (author of the second Gospel) preached in Alexandria, and so the church is called St. Mark's Church. We were among the first people to accept Christianity, even before the Catholics. At one time, the Coptic Orthodox Christian Church was persecuted, but its members were steadfast and unwavering in their beliefs.

The persecution started when the church was divided. The Catholics started selling places in paradise. They said that you could pay to have your sins forgiven and go to heaven. The Coptic Orthodox Church was very upset with this and became divided. The Orthodox Church is very steadfast; anyone who changes a word in the Bible is no longer considered Orthodox and can be rejected from the church.

We do not change our Bible; it has been the same since the birth of Jesus. We have the Old Testament and the New Testament, each written by many different authors. But all were given their words by God. Therefore, we cannot change even one word.

I read the Bible now in both Arabic and English, but until age eighteen I could read it only in English because of my schooling. Later, when I wanted to serve the Lord by speaking about him to Arabic people, I learned how to read the Bible in Arabic. Now that I'm older I like the big Bibles with the biggest print. I have many, many Bibles and give them to people.

In Arabic, the Lord is "al Rabb." We do not call him only "Jesus;" I like to say "the Lord Jesus." I am proud that Jesus came to my country; this is even mentioned in the Bible. The teachers in the English Mission College told us Jesus Christ escaped to Egypt and that we were lucky as Egyptians because Jesus came to our country. He said "blessed be Egypt my people."

There are seven churches in Cairo built near places that Jesus visited. Everybody visits them and knows that Jesus lived here for many months. He went to a monastery in Upper Egypt and stayed for a couple of months. At one such place, Jesus and his mother were thirsty and drank from a well. The tree of Miriam in Mattaria marks a place where Jesus and his followers lived for some time.

Christianity is my life, and my goal is to serve the people like Jesus did. Jesus was peaceful and wants us to live peacefully. I do not worry about what I will eat, drink, or wear. I care only that the poor will eat, that they have homes. I have rooms for the poor to live in so they can have shelter.

Jesus is from the East, so he looked like us. I once visited Bethlehem while on a church tour to Cyprus. The leader asked us if we would like to go on a twenty-four-hour tour to the Holy Land. We went to Bethlehem and visited all the churches and places where the Lord Jesus went, where he prayed, and where drops of his blood spilled in agony to save us from our sins. To see this was magnificent! We kneeled where baby Jesus' cradle had been, went to the church where the ascension took place, and saw the tomb. We walked the same road Jesus did with the cross, took the same steps he took.

I am sure Jesus would be sorry for what is going on in the Holy Land today; he is the Prince of Peace. He came to the world to give peace, but now it is all bloodshed.

Christians are upset about what is happening in the Holy Land, but to them there is no solution except that Jesus will come and the world will end. But in reality, there is hope for everybody if they will open their hearts; if they harden their hearts there will be no solution.

I don't know why people in the West worry about how many will go to heaven and how many will not. Each one must look at himself or herself and ask, "Am I ready to meet Jesus in his second coming?" He will accept anyone no matter if they are Muslim, Jew, or Christian. We will not go to heaven because of our works; we are going to heaven by the blood of Jesus who saved us from our sins, and because we love and serve him.

What is this strange talk about some big explosion (and rapture) that the evangelicals talk about? He said he is going to come and take his loved ones to heaven. Those that accept him as savior will go with him to heaven, even those in the grave who will arise.

I do not want anyone to know me for my works. It is enough that God knows me, knows I love Him. He said that what you do for the poor you do for me.

I do not think I could live without religion. Religion must be taught in school because it makes life real, gives purpose to life. My school was an English missionary college and taught religion even though the government didn't want religion to be taught in schools. The school told the government and King Farouq, "We are missionaries; we came from England to teach religion in school. If you don't want religion in school, we will close the school." So they kept religion in my school. Then the government said that the Quran must be taught in school. The missionaries refused to teach the Quran, so many Muslim students left the English Mission College.

The Muslims at the school did not mind learning the Bible. We were all friendly and we all learned about Christianity. No one was forced to be a Christian, but all were told to spread the words in the Bible because it is true and it changes lives. Egypt will never remove religion from schools, because Egypt has real Christians and good Muslims who have faith.

*   *   *

I am very happy that I was born in Egypt. I love Egypt. It has many poor people that I can help. There are many people who left Egypt and immigrated to Canada, America, and elsewhere. I feel these people are rather selfish; Egyptians should stay here and work here and help the poor by any means because it is our duty to serve our country and fellow Egyptians who need us. If all educated [Egyptians] emigrate to America or Canada, who will be left here? The best leave—doctors, engineers, scientists. We need our people to remain here and serve their country.

People in my community help me serve. I have two doctors, two engineers, and others who graduated from college. If I feel a person is sick, I call the volunteers and ask if they will please come and help us, which they happily do. Going to clubs and parties, thinking about what I'm going to wear, keeping up with the latest fashion—these things are not what I enjoy doing now.

It helps that in Egypt we can practice the religion we want. The church is just across from my house and every day they have a mass. I go each week to have communion.

I have ten volunteers who sort out donated clothes, reselling the new ones to raise funds for our projects and giving the used ones to the poor. Twenty volunteers help me with outside work, like feeding the poor and doing home visits. One volunteer told me about some families that had no food at all, so we give them monthly salaries to buy food. On Christmas and Easter we give one chicken to families of four and two chickens to families of six.

We also help poor children pay school tuition; I had many calls at the beginning of this school year asking for help in paying tuition. All they need is 100 Egyptian pounds[10] per year, while the rich kids pay 15,000 pounds a year. I ask my Sunday School students, "Can you imagine that these poor boys need only 100 pounds a year, but cannot afford it?" If I don't pay it for them, they cannot enter school. Sometimes they cannot even afford pencils.

About 150 handicapped poor get clothes from me. I also have many widows who rely on me, and even people who were well off but suddenly found themselves very poor when life became expensive or the husband went blind and could no longer work. We even help young people who want to get married and cannot afford it. Anybody who asks receives, and everything is in

---

[10] 100 Egyptian pounds is equal to about US$20. Education in Egypt is free, but students must pay registration fees.

prayer. I pray, "Lord Jesus, guide me so that I give to the right person, the right amount, the right clothes."

*   *   *

I visited America only once many years ago when my brother lived in California; I was there for forty-five days. It is gorgeous and you can find everything in plenty, but this is not what I care for; I wouldn't think of ever going back again. I love to serve my people. I know that there are poor people in California and in America, but there are also more people there who can talk to them about Jesus.

Many Americans are hardening their hearts, and it's the most dangerous thing. They are so busy with making money, working, buying houses—just like what is happening now to rich people in Egypt. I worry about them and pray for them. I was listening to a sermon yesterday on what happens when people put their hearts in money. It is dangerous, because you forget about the poor people. But I'm doing something good; I am trying to collect money from the rich to help the poor.

I don't care very much for the U.S. government, I'm sorry to say. They are involved in too many things, too many wars. There is one solution to end fighting: if every person helps as many people as they can. Nobody that does bad things, like the U.S. government, and hardens his heart, can be in heaven with the Lord.

I helped a girl enter university this year. She begged me to help her because no one in her family ever has attended university. I told her, "Since you really want to go we will pay the tuition for one year, and you must try and enter Cairo University next year." Cairo University has free education. Later she told me she was cold, so I sent her blankets and clothes. Why can't all the people of the world do the same and help young people go to college?

I'm serving people who don't have a home. I thank God every time I have a shower with hot water. You would think that everybody has hot water, but most of the people I help do not; most don't even have a water tap! They carry pots to get government water from the end of the street. These are the people whom Jesus says are your brothers and sisters. Are you serving these people? Are you trying to help them be happy? I feel sorry for you if you aren't.

God is always supplying me with what I need to pay for the poor; money comes in miraculous ways. There is a very strange story that perhaps is not so strange after all, as God always does strange things. A nun came to me and said she wanted to help two families that had nothing to eat. The women were widows with three children, two of them handicapped. Later, the nun called again and said that she found more widowed women with kids and no money. We calculated how much we should spend and it turned out that for all of them we needed 950 pounds. The nun was astounded when I told her how much we would be giving these families. She knew that this money was what we had put aside to pay school fees for some students. I told her the Lord would provide, that what we pay he gives back in abundance. I assured her that I had done this before and everything would work out.

I gave her the 950 pounds—and this was back when our budget was only a few hundred pounds per month; now we have a monthly budget of thousands. After she left, I had a telephone call from one of my friends to tell me that new clothes had come in from London, clothes we could sell at our bazaar. My friend sent the clothes with her husband, and to my surprise I found an envelope in the bag; she hadn't mentioned an envelope. I opened it and found 950 pounds. I was astounded! I screamed, "I thank you Lord, thank you Lord!"

I called my friend to thank her for sending the money. She told me that the previous night an acquaintance who rarely visited had stopped by her house, given her the envelope, and asked her to give it to a lady who does very trustworthy work.

I called the nun and asked her if she had distributed the money yet. She said she was on her way to do so, and told me how happy the widows would be. I told her that the 950 pounds had already come back to me; the Lord had sent the money before she even started distributing it!

This was a lesson from the Lord: He provides everything in abundance. Never did I need a chicken that didn't come; never did I need money for school fees that didn't come. And what comes I give; I give what's needed.

If all the people of the world would give to the poor we would all be okay and pleasing to the Lord.

I would like to ask the American people this: Do we thank the Lord enough for allowing us to live in clean homes, go to good schools, have the opportunity to eat what we want, go to picnics and on vacation, when there are people in the world—our brothers and sisters—who have nothing to eat except a few loaves of bread?

These are the people that we all need to be serving.
I am responsible for serving the poor in Egypt; you are responsible for serving those near you. Why can't we all live by this concept?

Conclusion

The most important conclusion of this book is that ordinary Arabs and Americans want dialogue between the two peoples. This is evident in the questions posed by Americans and the frank and open Arab answers. Indeed, more than voices were heard in this exchange—a connection was made between hearts and minds from two cultures.

Another powerful conclusion is that Arabs like Americans, but Arabs frequently do not like the policies and actions of the U.S. government. An important lesson contained in these interviews is that—contrary to same American news media and conservative pundits—most Arabs condemned the tragic events of September 11th, 2001. An important theme in the interviews is that solving the "Palestinian Problem" is the key to peace in the Middle East, and America has the power to turn the key—if only she will accept the challenge. An inescapable conclusion, one that may surprise American readers, is that the Arabs interviewed believe they receive more objective news than Americans do.

Throughout the interviews the American reader may have noticed other surprises. Many Arabs are Christian and many believe in religious tolerance. Both the Arab Christians and the Arab Muslims interviewed see a strong kinship between "the people of the book"—Muslims, Christians, and Jews. Not only did the interviewees condemn the September 11th attacks, they hated that these attacks were associated with Islam. Most decried any kind of religious extremism, as well as terrorism aimed at civilians. Finally, the Arab interviewees were often mercilessly self-critical. They hungered for political change and challenged the U.S. to foster democracy in the region—but through diplomacy and even economics, not through the barrel of a gun. They invited our leadership by example—not by invasion.

Arabs Like Americans—*But Not The American Government*

Not one single Arab I met during my two months in the Middle East held individual Americans responsible for U.S. foreign policy toward the Arab world and Muslims. Not one single person uttered a negative word about American people as individuals. No one made fun of Americans or was sarcastic or ridiculed their mannerisms or culture. On the contrary, there was much admiration for the American people, as reflected in the interviews. Indeed, several of the Arab interviewees said that *only* the American people can save and preserve the ideal America that so many people in the world look up to. Many Arabs believe that Americans need to know more about their own government's practices in the Arab world before they judge why Arabs behave the way they do.

The twelve subjects and everyone else I met in Egypt, Jordan, and Kuwait condemned the September 11th , 2001 attacks on the U.S. This should be a clear answer to some propagandists in the American media who keep repeating that not enough Arabs and Muslims condemned these acts. The twelve respondents were also extremely upset by the negative consequences that the September 11th tragedy had on Islam and Arabs—so much so that they expressed doubts that only Osama bin Laden and a few amateurs were involved in plotting the acts.

Americans and Arabs Need to Communicate

The twelve subjects show that the Arab people have a variety of opinions about important issues, just like any other vibrant people in the world. The respondents all asked Americans to make an effort to learn more about Arab history, politics, language, food, culture, and customs before pointing fingers at such a proud people with so much history. Americans need to learn this from Arabs themselves or from credible American Arabs and experts who do not have hidden agendas to destroy any attempts to foster coexistence between Arabs and Americans. We need, as West and East, a dialogue—not a clash.

Palestine—The "Sore Spot" of the Arab World

A second significant lesson pervaded the interviews—the heart of economic and political problems in the Arab world is the issue of Palestine. The American government might continue to ignore this fact, but the American people cannot afford to ignore it any longer. Almost all of the twelve participants considered Palestine to be the thorniest issue for Muslim and Christian Arabs alike. The United States government's unconditional support for the State of Israel causes tremendous animosity in Arab nations, especially when it is compounded with an inconsistent policy for dealing with the legitimate human and national rights of the Palestinian people.

Extremists like Osama bin Laden twist and abuse the legitimate cause of the Palestinians—to their detriment. Many Arabs believe—as demonstrated in the interviews in this book—that justly solving the Palestinian problem will render such abuse by extremists obsolete. Most importantly, is there a reason for Americans to begin educating themselves on the question of Palestine? Is there a reason for Americans to ask their government to handle this issue even-handedly? Yes, according to the interviewees—most said that every American needs to know more about the Palestinians and this problem. But what can we, as Americans, do about the Palestinian problem?

"Everything!" said the interviewees. Without exception they said that the key to peace in the Middle East was the American people. Speaking from their own hearts—directly to American hearts—with no governments or media in between to muffle their voices, they expressed the same heartfelt truth: If Americans know more about the reality and hopes and dreams of the Palestinians—Americans will force their government to be more even-handed and fair to all parties.

Speaking directly to American hearts, in admiration of America's people, accomplishments, and democracy—the interviewees made only one request: Learn about us! And then decide for yourselves whether your government and president are doing the right thing about the Palestinians.

American Jews should not feel threatened by Arab compassion for the Palestinians. Instead, they should understand that the twelve people interviewed were asking for a *just solution* for the Palestinians that also guarantees Israel's *security* and rights. Therefore, American Jews should encourage more dialogue between Palestinians and Israelis. As witnessed in this book, many Christian and Muslim Arabs who live in the region today still fervently hope for and believe that the Israelis and Palestinians can settle their differences.

We all should help play the role of peacemakers because, whether we like it or not, Israelis and Palestinians are in this together from now on. Neither the Palestinians nor the Israelis will "go away." No amount of wars or walls will ever rid the world of either people. Therefore, all of us—Arabs, Palestinians, Israelis, and Americans—need to face this reality and try to make the best of the situation.

How Arabs View the Iraq War

The interviewees differed in their opinions on the invasion of Iraq. Hamed and Haifa in neighboring Kuwait understandably supported the removal of Saddam Hussein from power and hoped that American troops would not leave before the U.S. secures a stable Iraq. Yet they expressed horror at the U.S. mismanagement of Iraq after the collapse of the Hussein regime.

Others interviewed completely opposed the Iraq War—not because they supported Saddam, but because they believed it was an illegal war fought under a thick fog of blatant lies. To most Arabs, the invasion of Iraq reinforced the belief that America preaches *selective* freedom, morality, and democracy. Young Muhamed eloquently drew an analogy between two authoritarian leaders: Saddam Hussein (whom the U.S. first built up and then destroyed) and Muammar Qaddafi of Libya (whom the U.S. long vilified, but now approves of). He pointed out that the U.S. government and others in the West are hypocritical in dealing so differently with these two authoritarian leaders. Some of the twelve respondents even expressed a fear that the current American foreign policy in the region would exacerbate terrorism rather than eliminate it.

Most of the interviewees reached the conclusion that oil was a major cause of the Iraq War. Yet the Iraq War was not perceived by them primarily as a means for the U.S. government to secure its need for oil, but rather as a way to enforce U.S. hegemony on the world. In other words: whoever controls the oil controls the world.

From the interviews, the American invasion of Iraq appears still fresh in the minds of people in the Arab nations. Despite President Bush's statement of "mission accomplished," the Iraq War rages on daily in the Arab news media. Yet, the twelve interviewees were nearly unanimous in their view that the daily oppression and uncertain future of Palestine is what irks the people most in Arab nations.

They are convinced that the Palestinian-Israeli conflict should require more American attention and involvement in the peace process. Isn't this remarkable? Americans are still seen by Arabs in the region as potentially the deciding factor in peacemaking between the Palestinians and Israelis. But the U.S. has thus far failed to accept this challenge. The interviewees would like to know why.

Arabs Take a Critical Look at Themselves

The other most pressing issue after Palestine that emerged in the interviews was the lack of true democracy anywhere in the Arab world. In this vein, the interviewees were just as critical of their own governments and political systems as they were of the

United States government and its policies in the region. Most agreed that something must be done about leaders who stay in power for too long. Several said that constitutions of Arab nations need to be rewritten to guarantee that a leader can be voted out as easily as he can be voted in. Again, opinions varied between those who did not mind American and European democratic models and those who favored a homegrown type of democracy. However, most agreed that Arab democracy should and will only happen through evolution—not revolution. A truly sad feeling expressed by the interviewees was that most did not expect democracy to happen in their lifetimes, except for young Muhamed who said that it would not happen until he is in his sixties!

Most of the twelve interviewees criticized the United States for supporting dictators and authoritarian regimes. Many were amazed at how many Americans did not realize that it was their tax money that financed Osama bin Laden and the fundamentalist Mujahideen in Afghanistan during the 1980s. Many were shocked that the Bush administration's concept of bringing freedom to Iraq also included banning *al Jazeera,* the television news service considered by many Arabs to be the only free media in that part of the world. Indeed, today most people in the Arab world attribute any democratic change currently happening as being inspired by *al Jazeera*'s news coverage.

Differing Views on Arab Culture, Religion, and Language

The opinions of the twelve respondents differed on the teaching of religion in schools. Some staunchly advocated its continuance, often with the condition that schools teach about all three "people of the book"—meaning Islam and the two other major monotheistic religions: Christianity and Judaism. Others favored a total revamp of all studies to make Arab schools consistent with their Western counterparts—but without tampering with the teachings of Islam or Arab values. Most expressed the need to separate church and state.

Almost all the respondents stressed that what makes an Arab is the Arabic language and family kinship. Some complained that family ties were sometimes a little too close, yet all agreed that the family was the core of Arab society and helped define what it means to be an Arab. This is another way that Arabs and Americans could communicate better—reading about the trials and tribulations of families in each other's countries.

This leads me to suggest that Arab academic institutions need to translate into English the wealth of novels written by Arab authors and make them available to Western audiences. There is an ongoing endeavor to do so, but its success will require financing by philanthropic organizations and perhaps even government grants.

When an American reads the intricate and often funny details of the daily lives of ordinary Egyptians, Iraqis, or Syrians, this will create a more human understanding of the worries, dreams, expectations, and frustrations in the minds of these people. Just as in the twelve interviews herein, reading Arab authors emphasizes a universal truth: Most people are basically the same everywhere—decent, hard-working, and family-oriented. Unfortunately, their governments are too often the opposite. As Haifa so eloquently said, the Arabic culture is rich in all aspects— food, music, literature, science—and had Arabs been freer they would have invented more and created more.

I would urge Arab-Americans to pay attention to the sushi phenomenon in the U.S. where Japan is now more associated with gourmet food than with their attack on Pearl Harbor. There is a lesson here for Arab-Americans—it might take *hummus* and *tablouleh* to change the image of Arabs. Arab Americans need their own *Cosby Show* and their own *My Big Fat Arabic Wedding*.

Change is Needed in the Arab World

From the twelve men and women in this book, one might get the impression that Arabs have achieved much as individuals in every corner of the world, but collectively have failed to take their rightful place on the world stage—so far. One gets the feeling that it is time for every Arab to have an individual awakening—each person starting with his or herself and then turning to family. The observations made by the diverse interviewees lead to an inescapable conclusion—moving forward is a matter of survival, and Arabs need to start seriously questioning the lack of democratic practices at home, in schools, in the workplace, and in government.

Intellectuals in the Arab world face severe adversity in presenting new ideas and debating change—but it is my feeling that they need to persevere in these efforts. Similarly, Arab media could do a great deal to discover and present the concerns of average people in the Arab nations. I am certain that there are many citizens in Egypt, Algeria, Jordan, Morocco, Syria, Kuwait, Palestine, Lebanon and all of the Arab nations who want their voices heard locally and beyond. Journalists can help stimulate such a free political and religious discourse. The twelve interviewees clearly demonstrated that Arabs are already thinking democratically and are open to debate and broad-based discussions.

*   *   *

By creating this book, I have tried to bring the Arab and American peoples a step closer to beginning a dialogue—exchanging ideas, values, and questions. I ask American readers to answer the questions posed by the twelve interviewees and to e-mail them to samarjar@sunline.net.

Any failure in reaching my objective is solely my responsibility. Any success achieved by the book in promoting mutual understanding I attribute to the many people who posed the questions and, of course, to those who answered them.

Appendix A

Appendix A:

Questions from Americans to Arabs

The following question guide has been divided into two parts: Appendix A—Questions from Americans to Arabs, and Appendix B—Questions from Arabs to Americans. The questions for Arabs were the basis for the interviews contained in this book. Not all questions were asked of each interviewee; I made an attempt to distribute the questions evenly.

It seemed some issues were recurrent, however, and when a topic came up I felt obligated to ask the relevant questions from Americans, whether I had planned to ask those particular questions of that interviewee or not.

This part of the guide has been divided into seven categories:
1. Religion
2. Women in the Arab world
3. Israel and Palestine
4. The Relationship between the United States and the Middle East
5. The War in Iraq
6. September 11th
7. Arab and Muslim Society

You will find that some questions appear in more than one category. This is because, as is true everywhere, most issues involve numerous elements (religion, culture, government, etc.) and cannot be given just one label.

Not every question that was asked is answered within this book. However, it is important that Arabs know what questions Americans have, whether they are able to answer all of them or not. Perhaps some of these unanswered questions will promote future thought and help foster continued dialogue.

Religion

*Is Osama bin Laden truly religious—or does he use religion
for political ends?*

Do Muslim women feel that their religion has been a source of
comfort and support for them throughout their lives, and do they
believe that it will lead to a better life for them after they die?

Is "knowing" the same to you as "believing," and if not, what is
the difference? If you cannot "know" that your faith is true, how
can you insist that it is?

Are there many versions of the Quran or just one "true one?"

What do you believe regarding religions—all religions? Do you
believe they are helpful or harmful to humankind? Tell me why
you believe as you do?

Since there are a variety of religions, would it not be wise to take
religion out of government, so that all people could benefit
regardless of religious beliefs?

What role should Islam play in the governments of Arab countries?

Islam and Terrorism

Where in the Quran does it say that you shall kill and hate us?

What are the root causes that stimulate Muslims to turn to
terrorism in so many countries throughout the world?

What is being done in the religious schools to manage the extremist positions that are creating belief systems among the young that may work against a peaceful future?

I would like to know why all prominent Arab clerics did not and still do not unequivocally condemn the murder of over 3,000 Americans on September 11th. The reaction after this slaughter was lukewarm at best. If this had happened in the Arab world, the U.S. would have condemned it without reservation, and would have stepped forward to give whatever assistance it could.

Islam and the Outside World

If I do not believe in the God of Abraham, will you tolerate me (if I move to your country), including allowing me to participate in all aspects of civil life, such as government?

Do you think various religions should be taught in your schools as history so that children have a feel for other cultures?

What would it take for our two "worlds" (East/West, Muslim/Christian) to rediscover mutual respect and good will?

Do Muslims believe non-Muslims should be converted to Islam?

What can Humanists and those of other religions do, if anything, to get the tolerance and respect of Arab Muslims?

Have you ever heard of Jesus Christ?

Why do the fundamentalists have so much power over the rest of the Arab world?

Saudi Arabia and Wahabism

Americans are being told that children in Saudi Arabia are taught in their schools (including textbooks) that all non-Muslims are devils and the enemy. Is this true? If yes, what role does the Saudi Wahabi religious sect's viewpoint have in the Arab world?

Are the Saudis well thought of in the Arab world? Or are they respected only as the keeper of the two holy places, Mecca and Medina? Or both?

What are your thoughts about Wahabism?

Women in the Arab World

"How does it feel to live in a society where men are considered higher in status than women?"

What are your views about women?

What do you think women's roles should be in the family, in the workplace, in government, etc.?

Do you feel women are capable of doing what men can do?

How do you feel/believe women should dress?

Would you go to a woman doctor?

Do you think women should be doctors, lawyers, business people, etc.?

How do you feel about lesbian women and their role/rights in this world?

Who has the authority over a woman's body—the woman, church, or state?

Do Arab women feel happy that they were born in the Arab world, or do they sometimes wish they were born in another region?

Why do Arab men see women as objects.....not equal partners, with equal rights?

Israel and Palestine

Are you prepared to live with Israel as a neighbor?

What will it take for Arabs and Israelis to compromise and live in peace?

If you could solve the Israel/Palestine conflict today, how would you do it?
What can the American government do for the Arab world, Palestine in particular, that will help Arabs not to have hard feelings about the United States?

Is there room for Israel in the Middle East?

If the U.S. put pressure on Israel to make a lasting peace with the Palestinians, would this destroy support for al Qaeda?
Would the Muslim world's opinion of the U.S. change markedly (i.e. stop the very public anti-American displays, etc.) if American foreign policy toward Israel changed to a more neutral stance?
Is the Palestinian situation, in your belief, the major reason for most conflict and negative attitudes toward the U.S., or is it our interference in Middle Eastern politics that drives the divide between East and West?

208   Samar Dahmash-Jarrah

Why is it that we don't see more Arabs speaking out on the
Palestinian/Israeli conflict?

The Relationship Between the United States
and the Middle East

*What can we concerned Americans do to help mend the terrible rift
between us?*

Arab Views of America/Americans

Do you think America is going to try to indoctrinate your people
with our view of how the region should be? If so, how will the
Arab people react?

If I was to visit your countries, would you only see me as generic
American? Would I be safe?

What would be the three or four most important questions that
ordinary Arabs would like to ask ordinary Americans if they had
the chance to do so?

Do you believe the majority of Americans are anti-Arab?

Do you resent the United States? Why or why not?
What do you like most about the U.S.?

What do you dislike most about the U.S.?

Do you think the West overemphasizes the stereotypical social
status of the Arab world?

What are your expectations of the American government?

What are your expectations of the American people?

What questions would you have for me as an average American citizen?
How do you view the West and are there some things (culturally) that you can identify with?

Mending Relationships

How can America regain the trust of the Arab people after what we have done in Iraq?

What would we have to do to have the Arab world like us (besides not helping Israel)?

What would you like the relationship between the U.S. and the Arab/Muslim world to be, and do you believe it is achievable?

Will Arab people ever be able to forgive us when this nightmare that is upon us all is over?

Is the Palestinian situation, in your belief, the major reason for most conflict and the Arab attitude toward the U.S., or is it our interference in Middle Eastern politics that drives the divide between East and West?

What would it take for our two "worlds" (East/West, Muslim/Christian) to rediscover mutual respect and good will?

What would it take to totally and finally put an end to fighting with non-Arabs and would you be willing to do it?
Would the Muslim world's opinion of the U.S. change markedly (i.e. stop the very public anti-American displays, etc.) if American foreign policy toward Israel changed to a more neutral stance?

What needs to change for you to be comfortable with Americans and separately, America?

What can I, a seventy-year-old American woman, do to help heal the wounds between Americans and Arab Muslims and Muslims of other cultures throughout the world? What can I do as an individual so that we can live on the planet in peace together?

What one thing should the United States do to make the relationship between the U.S. and the Arab world a positive one and what should the people on both sides do to support that? What can the American government do for the Arab world, Palestine in particular, that will help Arabs not to have hard feelings about the United States?

How can people from Arab countries help turn the tide for the average American to see the love and compassion in the hearts of Arab people? Or better yet, how can we as Americans wipe away the rhetoric to better understand and be more ready to see the love? How will we ever be able to see the love in each other? Where is the love?

Presidential Issues

What would you like to tell President Bush?

What do you think of John Kerry?

Can you understand that despite the actions of our "leader," most Americans hold no animosity toward the people of the Arab world?

Can you forgive our people or do we have to live with the results of the sins of the administration?

Americans are being told by our President that Osama bin Laden and al Qaeda terrorists attacked the U.S. because they hate our freedom, democracy, and wealth. A minority viewpoint is that Arab terrorism against the U.S. and its allies is due to our policies in the Middle East. Which is true? If it's the policies, which ones do Arabs dislike?

The War in Iraq

Why is it that we don't see more Arabs speaking out against the situation in Iraq?

How can America regain the trust of the Arab people after what we have done in Iraq?

Where do you see the world's view of Iraq in the next few years?

What type of relationship do you think Iraq will have, diplomatically, with the U.S. when the conflict is over?

Which would you prefer to exist in Iraq, a theocracy or democracy?

Are you happy with the current leadership in Iraq? Would you vote to keep the current leadership in place?

Why are Iraqis killing Iraqis?

What was your reaction to the (Abu Ghraib) torture? What did you think of us before as compared to after?

How would you suggest solving the Iraq problem?

Should the U.S. bring the troops home immediately?

What do you think was the real reason for the invasion of Iraq?

Do you think that the U.S. will withdraw all of its troops from Iraq within 5 years, 10 years, ever?

Do you feel that U.S. troops should stay in Iraq?

What happened to freedom of the press? Why did they shut down al Jazeera in Iraq?

September 11th, 2001

If you were president of the United States during the September 11th, 2001 catastrophe, what would your response (militarily, economically, diplomatically, etc.) have been?

What series of U.S. policies or acts precipitated September 11th?

I would like to know why all prominent Arab clerics did not and still do not unequivocally condemn the murder of over 3,000 Americans on September 11th. The reaction after this slaughter was lukewarm at best. If this had happened in the Arab world, the U.S. would have condemned it without reservation, and would have stepped forward to give whatever assistance it could.

How should the United States government respond to attacks such as those on the World Trade Center and Pentagon on September 11th, 2001?

Americans are being told by President Bush that Osama bin Laden and al Qaeda terrorists attacked the U.S. because they hate our freedom, democracy, and wealth. A minority viewpoint is that Arab terrorism against the U.S. and its allies is due to our policies in the Middle East. Which is true? If it's the policies, which ones do Arabs dislike?

What would it take to totally and finally put an end to fighting with non-Arabs and would you be willing to do it?

If the U.S. put pressure on Israel to make a lasting peace with the Palestinians, would this destroy support for al Qaeda?
I know what you are willing to die for, but what will you live for?

Is Osama bin Laden truly religious—or does he use religion for political ends?

What are the root causes that stimulate Muslims to turn to terrorism in so many countries throughout the world?

What are your thoughts about bin Laden?

What is being done in the religious schools to manage the extremist positions that are creating belief systems among the young that may work against a peaceful future?

What did the instigators of September 11th hope to accomplish?

What should the U.S. do to avoid or prevent terrorism?

Arab and Muslim Society

I know what you are willing to die for, but what will you live for?

Cultural

Which, if any, writers and intellectuals from non-Arab countries
are held in high esteem by the general population in the Arab
world?

What are the expectations of you and your culture for a better
world now and in the future?

What things in your culture do you cherish and which one(s)
would you want to change?

What do you envision as the future of the Arab people?

Do you think the West overemphasizes the stereotypical social
status of the Arab world?

Do you think various religions should be taught in your schools as
history so that children have a feel for other cultures?

Why won't the Arab/Muslim world teach respect for human life,
freedom of speech and freedom of religion for ALL people?
If there is one thing you could say to the world about your
experience as an Arab, with the idea of love for humanity, what
would that one thing be?

As an Arab, what four values/ideas or things are the most
important to you in your life (in order from most to least
important)? Do you feel that people of most other cultures share
your feelings? Why or why not?

Political

What guiding principles would you most want to see adopted and followed by your government?

Do you believe that a system of government based on Western-style democracy and civil liberties is a practical option for the tribally-based societies of many Arab nations? If not, why not? If so, what is the single biggest challenge to democratic governance and how can it best be solved?

What percentage of the good things that happen to you are the result of domestic politics and what percentage are due to international politics?

What steps do Arab societies/governments need to take today in order to have another golden age where innovations and advances in the sciences, mathematics, arts, etc. flow forth abundantly from their lands, enriching the entire globe?

Daily Life

How do you prepare yourself, children, and the rest of the family when you leave home each day?

Are you happier today than you were last year?

Do you have hope for the future?

Have you ever read any of Ayn Rand's books?

Are you satisfied with your social status?

What crisis are you experiencing there?

How do you feel living in such an uncertain world, where you never know when you are going to lose your life, your home, and everything you have?

Regional Interactions

Are the Saudis well thought of in the Arab world or are they respected only as the keeper of the two holy places, Mecca and Medina? Or both?

Do you think Turkey is a "sell-out" or a Muslim country in development?
How do North African Arabs/Muslims view other Africans?

Who do you see as a person who could bring peace to the area?

What is the answer to not having any more wars in the Middle East?

What changes would you like to see in Arab countries (in your country)?

Americans are being told that children in Saudi Arabia are taught in their schools (including textbooks) that all non-Muslims are devils and the enemy. Is this true? If yes, what role does the Saudi Wahabi religious sect's viewpoint have in the Arab world?

Appendix B

Appendix B:

Questions from Arabs to Americans

This second part of the questions guide is listed by interview. These questions will help form the beginnings of a possible follow-up book, where Americans will answer Arab questions. Perhaps if you are an Arab reading this you have additional questions—or if you are American perhaps you'd like to help provide some answers.

Please go to www.ArabVoicesSpeak.com to respond.

Interview 1—Mohamed, Cairo, Egypt

1. What would it take for you to be interested in knowing more about us?
2. What can we do to get you to want to know more about us—to visit or read something about our history and culture?
3. I would like to see Americans interested in a television program about our country—about our problems and aspirations. What will it take for this to happen?

Interview 2—Kamil, Amman, Jordan

1. How can you support your president in such a baseless war (Iraq)? Every day brings evidence that proves the war was based on lies, and this evidence comes from Americans, historians, strategists, and intelligence experts.
2. How can you support such a war, but not find it in your heart to give that same level of support to resolving the Palestinian problem?

Interview 3—Enas, Cairo

1. The one question I have for the ordinary American is, "Don't you feel that America is becoming a tyrant and not applying justice toward other nations?"

Interview 4—Osama, Cairo

1. Why do people judge other people without really knowing them?
2. Why do Americans judge us without knowing us or even visiting us?

Interview 5—Hamed, Kuwait

1. I lived in America and I have many American friends, and I would like to ask each American a different question. I cannot just ask one question of all Americans; they are not all the same.

Interview 6—Hassan, Amman

1. Why did some Americans kill ordinary Muslims after September 11th?

Interview 7—Ola, Amman

1. Why do you find it too much for us to live like others?
2. Why do you want us to live inferior to others?
3. Why do you want us to die without exercising our right to self-defense?
4. Why is it too much for us to enjoy our natural wealth and resources that God gave us?

Interview 8—Khaled, Cairo

1. Why do you hate us?
2. Why do you only hear from one side? Why don't you listen to us?
3. Why don't you try to meet with us as we try to meet with you?

4. Why don't you allow us to explain our religion to you as you explain your ideologies and religion to us?

5. Why are you biased when it comes to Israel and forget that Palestinians are human beings who have the right to live freely, just as you do?

6. Why do you expect us to welcome your armies when you are destroying our mosques, schools, hospitals, and houses?

7. Why do Americans expect us to like their government when it supports undemocratic systems? Is it because you are not aware? Is it because you care only about your interests no matter at what cost they are fulfilled?

8. Do you really believe and trust that Bush is working for your interests, or do you think that he is seeking personal gains by finishing what his father failed to finish before him?

9. Do you really believe that the Bush administration has adequately justified the war against Iraq, or do you realize that you were as fooled as we were that there were weapons of mass destruction in Iraq? Where are those weapons now? How long will you wait for an answer?

Interview 9—Haifa, Kuwait

1. I would like to ask [Americans] if they really think the situation in Palestine is justified and that the U.S. is acting justly.

Interview 10—Mohamed, Cairo

1. When will you stop believing all you read in corporate-owned and newspapers see on TV?

Interview 11—Dr. Khaled, Amman

1. As a diplomat and a university professor, I would like to ask a question to American diplomats and professors: Can

you be objective and fair toward the Arab world? Can you be a pure American (one who does not always and unequivocally support Israel)?

Dr. Kahled's wife, Um Walid

1. I ask you [the author] as an American woman living in this time of terrorism and war, what authority do you have over your husband or son if they decide to go to war? How would you feel if they died in battle?
2. How do you feel when a Palestinian is killed by the Israeli army, or an Iraqi is killed?
3. How can you as a woman influence all these events and the decisions made by governments?

Interview 12—Madam Soad, Cairo

1. I am responsible for serving the poor in Egypt; you are responsible for serving those near you. Why can't we all live by this concept?

2. Do we thank the Lord enough for allowing us to live in clean homes, go to good schools, have the opportunity to eat what we want, go to picnics and on vacation, when there are people in the world—our brothers and sisters— who have nothing to eat except a few loaves of bread?

3. I helped a girl enter university this year... we will pay the tuition for one year. Later she told me she was cold, so I sent her blankets and clothes. Why can't all the people of the world do the same and help young people go to college?

Appendix C

Appendix C:

Resources

For more information about the topics discussed in this book please visit some of the websites listed below. They are a gateway for further learning about Arabs and Muslims in the U.S. and worldwide. More resource websites are tregularly added to the book's website. Please visit: www.ArabVoices.Speak.

Please note: Due to the ever-changing nature of the Internet some of these websites may not always be available. I apologize for any inconvenience this may cause.

Al-Ahram Weekly

http://weekly.ahram.org.eg
Al-Ahram Weekly is an independent English-language newspaper published in Egypt and widely read throughout the Arab world. First published in 1991, it provides English-language readers with objective, in-depth coverage of Egyptian and Arab politics, economy, culture, and society from an Egyptian perspective. Al-Ahram has hosted many leading international political commentators—both Arab and non-Arab—and regular contributors have included Noam Chomsky, Mohamed Hassanein Heikal, Edward Said, and Eric Rouleau.

     This website contains news, opinion, reader comments, and travel information.

American-Arab Anti-Discrimination Committee

www.adc.org
The American-Arab Anti-Discrimination Committee (ADC) is a civil rights organization committed to defending the rights of people of Arab descent and promoting their rich cultural heritage. The ADC, based in Washington, D.C., is the largest Arab-American grassroots organization in the United States. Founded in 1980 by U.S. Senator Jim Abourezk, the ADC welcomes people of

all backgrounds, faiths, and ethnicities. Advisory Board members include Muhammad Ali, Her Majesty Queen Noor, several U.S. Congressmen, Edward Said, and Casey Kasem, among many others.

Their website contains educational and legal resources, event listings, and information on political activism.

American Task Force on Palestine
www.americantaskforce.org
The American Task Force on Palestine (ATFP) is a non-partisan, not-for-profit corporation that seeks to promote awareness of the far-reaching benefits that Palestinian statehood will have for the U.S. in the areas of enhancing national security, furthering American values of freedom and democracy, and expanding economic opportunities throughout the Arab and Islamic worlds.

Their website contains news, a reading list, and printed and photo resources.

Americans for Peace Now
www.peacenow.org
Americans for Peace Now (APN) was founded in 1981 to support the activities of Shalom Achshav (Peace Now in Israel). APN, the leading U.S. advocate for peace in the Middle East, exists to help Israel and the Shalom Achshav movement achieve a comprehensive political settlement of the Arab-Israeli conflict consistent with Israel's long-term security needs and its Jewish and democratic values.

Their website contains publications, event listings and reviews, ways you can take action, and a free weekly e-mail newsletter.

Arab-American Action Network
www.aaiusa.org
Founded in 1985, the Arab American Institute (AAI) is a non-profit organization committed to the civic and political empowerment of Americans of Arab descent.

AAI enables Arab Americans to take increasingly visible and active roles in campaigns and elections by mobilizing resources, providing leadership development, working with party officials, electing delegates, and defining issues. Today, Arab American candidates and activists are involved at all levels - from school boards and judges to state officials and members of Congress. This success is a strong message that we are part of this country, and proud of the contributions we are making.

AAI campaign and election services include:

- Voter guides analyzing key federal races of interest to the community
- Congressional scorecards indicating how members vote on Arab American issues
- Voter mobilization materials such as bumper stickers, voter registration materials, voter lists, and get-out-the-vote guidelines
- Party conventions: Assistance and training for Arab Americans running for party delegates to national conventions, and organizing the Arab American presence at the national conventions.

Common Dreams
www.commondreams.org
Common Dreams is a national, non-profit citizens' organization working to unite progressive Americans and promote progressive visions for America's future. Founded in 1997, Common Dreams is committed to being on the cutting-edge of Internet use for

political organization and creating new models for Internet activism.

Their website contains an extensive news center, articles by well-known journalists, submission guidelines, and a free daily e-mail newsletter.

Council on American-Islamic Relations
www.cair-net.org
The Council on American-Islamic Relations (CAIR) exists to enhance understanding of Islam, encourage dialogue, protect civil liberties, empower American Muslims, and build coalitions that promote justice and mutual understanding. Established in 1994, CAIR is a nonprofit 501(c)(4), grassroots civil rights and advocacy group and America's largest Islamic civil liberties group. CAIR seeks to empower the American Muslim community and encourage their participation in political and social activism.

Their website contains action alerts, information on civil rights, publications, and a free daily e-mail newsletter.

Jewish Voice for Peace
www.jewishvoiceforpeace.org
Founded in 1996, Jewish Voice for Peace (JVP) is the voice of American Jews who support a peaceful resolution of the Israeli-Palestinian conflict and an end to Israel's occupation of Palestinian land. JVP has become the largest grassroots Jewish peace group in the U.S. and is guided by the principle that U.S. foreign policy must be based on promoting peace, democracy, human rights, and respect for international law.

Their website contains downloads, ways for you to take action, book and website resources, and a free monthly e-mail newsletter.

Palestine. Dying to Live.

www.dying2live.com

Palestine. Dying to Live. is a media campaign created by
Jordanian advertising and media professionals, writers, art
directors, and web developers to open the world's eyes to the
injustices and human rights violations committed against
Palestinians by Israeli occupation forces. The producers are
volunteers and not associated with any political party. Their goal
is simply to make the Western world aware of what is going on.

Their website contains information on the project and
downloadable images that you can use to help spread their
message.

Be Part of the Follow-up Book

Dear Reader—

I welcome your comments on this book and the views expressed herein by the subjects and the author.

You can be part of the follow-up book, tentatively titled *American Hearts Respond—Answers to Arab Questions.*

If you would like to help bring America and the Arab world closer together through dialogue and understanding, please contact me with your questions and/or answers for Arabs or Americans.

Please visit www.ArabVoicesSpeak.com for more details and contact information.

Samar Dahmash-Jarrah

Ordering Information

Arab Voices
speak to **American Hearts**

Cost

$15.95; e-mail samarjar@sunline.net for quantity discounts.

Shipping and handling

U.S.: Add $3.50 per book.

International: Please visit www.ArabVoicesSpeak.com to place international orders.

Please enclose a check or money order payable to Olive Branch Books and mail to:

Olive Branch Books
12776 Westwood Lakes Blvd.
Tampa, FL 33626

Number of copies _____ x US $15.95   = _____

Shipping (see rates above)   + _____

TOTAL ENCLOSED   = _____

SHIP TO:

Name: _____

Address: _____

City: _____ State: _____ Zip: _____

Country: _____ Telephone: (_____) _____

If being sent as a gift, please add *From:* _____

Index

God, 22, 28, 30, 38, 45, 51, 59, 62, 63,
   80, 81, 86, 89, 92, 93, 102, 107,
   108, 113, 117, 118, 119, 120, 122,
   123, 124, 125, 169, 179, 180, 182,
   184, 186, 187, 202, 216
Government, 191
Gulf War, 65

H

Hajj, 72
Hilda Polat, 7
Hollywood, 67, 127
Holocaust, 83, 125
Human Rights, 193
Husbands, 175

I

India, 6, 76, 78
Indonesia, 16, 168, 172
Intellectuals, 197
Internet, IV, VI, 95, 96, 149, 220, 222
Iran, 8, 16, 76
Iraq, 9, 8, 9, 10, 11, 12, 15, 19, 23, 26,
   31, 32, 52, 53, 65, 66, 76, 80, 82,
   94, 95, 100, 110, 111, 119, 131,
   134, 135, 145, 146, 150, 158, 159,
   170, 171, 173, 193, 194, 195, 200,
   206, 208, 209, 215, 217
Iraq War, 9, 8, 31, 66, 171, 193, 194
Islam, III, IV, V, 3, 9, 16, 22, 37, 38,
   41, 44, 53, 93, 99, 102, 103, 104,
   105, 115, 117, 118, 119, 121, 123,
   124, 125, 126, 128, 130, 131, 139,
   140, 141, 142, 153, 165, 168, 172,
   173, 175, 190, 191, 195, 201, 202,
   222
Islamic, 3, 5, 16, 25, 38, 40, 45, 50, 51,
   52, 60, 63, 80, 101, 103, 104, 105,
   117, 127, 141, 167, 221, 222
Israel, 3, 11, 12, 8, 9, 10, 31, 51, 52, 54,
   61, 75, 79, 80, 82, 83, 84, 108, 111,
   112, 130, 131, 143, 145, 156, 157,

166, 169, 173, 174, 192, 193, 200,
   204, 206, 210, 217, 218, 221, 223
Italian, 5, 13
Italy, 61, 165

J

Jesus Christ, 21, 61, 62, 86, 87, 92, 96,
   179, 182, 202
Jewish, III, IV, 5, 80, 108, 143, 157,
   173, 221, 223
Jews, III, 51, 62, 83, 84, 108, 109, 110,
   122, 124, 125, 126, 143, 157, 173,
   174, 190, 193, 223
Jordan, VII, IX, X, 9, 11, 18, 19, 20,
   21, 23, 27, 31, 48, 61, 89, 90, 91,
   92, 93, 94, 95, 96, 98, 99, 100, 101,
   102, 103, 105, 106, 113, 163, 164,
   165, 166, 167, 168, 169, 170, 173,
   174, 175, 215, 216, 217
Jordanian, 20, 21, 24, 27, 89, 91, 92,
   100, 101, 103, 163, 164, 165, 166,
   168, 172, 175, 224

K

Kabul, 80
Killing, 25
King Hussein, 20, 21, 91, 163
Kingdom, 78
Korea, 9
Kuwait, VII, IX, 9, 11, 59, 71, 73, 75,
   76, 77, 78, 81, 91, 115, 133, 134,
   135, 136, 137, 138, 139, 140, 141,
   142, 145, 146, 170, 193, 216, 217

L

Language, 195
Latin America, 9
Lebanese, 5, 10, 73, 135, 196
Lebanese Civil War, 73
Lebanon, VII, X, 48, 73, 82, 110, 135

Q

Qatar, 10
Queen Noor, 20, 221
Quran, 16, 80, 81, 86, 92, 104, 117,
119, 120, 121, 122, 124, 125, 141,
152, 153, 173, 184, 201

R

Ramadan, 22, 116, 178
Red Sea, 138
Relationships, 206
Religion, 50, 51, 62, 118, 130, 140,
184, 195, 200, 201
Republicans, 65, 72
Resources, 12, 220
Revolution, 135, 153
Russia, 9, 12, 170

S

Saud family, 79
Saudi Arabia, X, 4, 32, 76, 77, 78, 79,
80, 81, 85, 86, 91, 93, 122, 172,
174, 203, 213
Science, 117, 118, 121
Senator, 20, 220
Senegal, 61
September 11th, V, VII, 9, 24, 26, 29,
50, 55, 61, 65, 79, 81, 93, 94, 96,
99, 100, 109, 111, 115, 125, 126,
127, 143, 144, 158, 168, 169, 172,
190, 191, 200, 202, 209, 210, 216
Shiite, 139
Sinai, 108, 156
Socialism, 43
Sorry Law, 38
Soviet Union, 50, 143, 158
Spain, 6, 125
State Department, U.S., 89, 120, 193
Sudan, 4, 122
Suicide, 107
Sunnah, 117

Sunni, 103
SUVs, 100
Sweden, 13
Switzerland, 61, 83
Syria, 6, 8, 48, 75, 164

T

Taliban, 93, 136, 158
Tawator, 120
Tax, 101, 112
Technology, 118
Television, IX, 6, 10, 19, 29, 35, 56,
73, 74, 91, 110, 116, 118, 125, 126,
127, 149, 159, 160, 217
Terrorism, 51, 201
Textbooks, 135
Third World, 63, 167, 169
Tibetan, 9
Tunis, 6
Turkey, 6, 16, 79, 172, 213
Turkish, 71
Turks, 46

U

United Kingdom, 15
United Nations, 28, 31, 32, 66, 167
United States., IX, 3, 9, 10, 12, 6, 7, 8,
10, 11, 12, 13, 15, 16, 20, 23, 24,
25, 26, 28, 29, 30, 31, 32, 47, 52,
61, 71, 73, 75, 76, 80, 81, 82, 83,
84, 85, 86, 89, 90, 91, 93, 94, 99,
100, 110, 111, 112, 119, 120, 122,
127, 133, 136, 141, 143, 144, 146,
149, 151, 155, 158, 166, 167, 168,
169, 170, 171, 174, 178, 186, 190,
191, 192, 193, 194, 195, 196, 197,
202, 204, 205, 206, 207, 208, 209,
210, 217, 220, 221, 223, 227
University of Cairo, 5, 60
USA PATRIOT Act, 23

V

Vatican, 27
Vietnam, 16, 61
Violence, 24, 52
Voting, 12

W

Wahabism, 172, 173, 203, 213
War, 9, 8, 23, 31, 65, 66, 73, 156, 171,
193, 194, 200, 208
Washington, D.C., 137, 220
Watergate, 71, 73, 74

West, the, 15, 20, 23, 24, 49, 67, 71,
79, 80, 85, 86, 139, 159, 171, 175,
195, 196, 212, 224
Women's Issues, 10, 37, 38, 39, 40, 41,
42, 44, 47, 48, 49, 56, 85, 104, 105,
106, 115, 135, 136, 137, 138, 141,
142, 154, 164, 174, 175, 187, 196,
201, 203, 204
World War II, 30, 64, 156, 158, 167

Z

Zimbabwe, 8
Zionism, 83, 166, 171
Zionists, III, 84, 130, 166, 168, 169,
170